BILL MAHER

And His Favorite Bible Stories

Mike Minter

Dedication

To Prime Time
The greatest adult Sunday school class on the planet

Acknowledgments

I have been encouraged by friends to pursue this writing. I thank my publisher, McGilligan Publishing, and particularly Margaret Johnson, Jane Foster and Charles Smith for patiently navigating me through this world of writing. Jenniffer Milligan, Jess Jordan, and Lyndi Harris have helped me negotiate the messy world of computers.

About the Author

Mike Minter has been a pastor for over fifty years. He and his wife Kay planted Reston Bible Church in 1975. The church grew rapidly into a large church by the grace of God. Over the forty-seven years of the church's existence, RBC has given heavily to world missions around the globe. Mike has made over thirty-five mission trips to various parts of the world. Mike and Kay are now deeply involved in Rolling Hills Community Church in Franklin, Tennessee, where Mike is a part-time staff member. He is also the author of *Stay the Course: A Pastor's Guide to Navigating the Restless Waters of Ministry.*

Foreword

It has been said, "There are no atheists in a foxhole." When bombs are going off, and one's life is in danger, and war is all around, people often turn to God. However, most of life is not lived in that metaphorical foxhole. Most of life is lived above ground, plodding through the regular routines of everyday life.

For the average person just trying to get ahead, making a living, raising a family, and enjoying life, what would move him or her Godward? In other words, if a crisis doesn't nudge a person toward God, what will? Answer: truth, reason, and understanding.

A person can actually come to faith in God, and His Son, Jesus Christ, through the exercise of one's intellect. Don't misunderstand me—I'm not saying that coming to faith is entirely an intellectual exercise. We must never discount the work of God's Spirit in "wooing" unbelievers and opening "the minds of their hearts."

But all too often we think that all we need to do in coming to faith in God is to "just believe." We tend to dismiss the importance of reason and intellect in that process. Yet reason and intellect are some of the very attributes that God has given us that allow us to believe in Him and connect with Him.

Intellect and faith are not mutually exclusive terms, despite what the "Bill Mahers" of the world would have you to believe. There is such a thing as intelligent faith! In fact, God even invites people to exercise intelligent faith when He says through the pen of the prophet Isaiah, "Come now, let us reason together" (Isa. 1:18).

In the first century AD, the apostle Paul took the same approach with the people of his day. Acts 17:17 records that Paul "reasoned in the synagogue with the Jews and with the Gentile worshipers, and in the marketplace daily with those who happened to be there" (NKJV).

Paul wasn't afraid to engage the atheist, the pagan, or the agnostic. On the contrary, he traveled the known world looking for such people in order to persuade them about the love of God and the person of Jesus Christ. Some believed, some did not. But Paul died a martyr's death defending this truth, as have countless other Christian martyrs around the world over the last twenty-one centuries.

In the style of the apostle Paul, Mike Minter is appealing to the skeptics and atheists of our day, too. He is engaging our God-given intellect and calling us to exercise reason throughout the pages that follow. In the more than two decades that I have known him, Pastor Mike has demonstrated a sincere desire to see people come to faith in Jesus—not with blind faith, but with intelligent faith. This book is consistent with that lifelong mission of his.

Perhaps it is not a coincidence that you have picked up this book or received it as a gift from someone. No matter how you may have come to possess it, today is an opportunity for you to engage both the heart and the mind in discovering or rediscovering truth.

Since we are living in such a relative time of "my truth" and "your truth," it is vitally important for people to know THE truth—the Bible—God's love letter to a lost world. I trust that whether you are an atheist who is seeking, or a Christian who is believing, this book will prompt you to read THE Book and to know the One reflected from Genesis to Revelation—Jesus Christ, God's Son.

Gary Hamrick

Senior Pastor, Cornerstone Chapel,
Leesburg, VA

Preface

Having been a pastor for over fifty years, there is precious little I haven't seen or experienced. I had the privilege of founding a church in Northern Virginia with my wife Kay in 1975. By God's amazing grace, the church grew quickly, and we became a megachurch in a very short period of time. Since we were about twenty miles from Washington DC, I had access to non-classified information from high-level government employees, as well as admirals and generals who attended regularly.

Some in our congregation met with the President on a daily basis. There were others who briefed military officers in the War Room at the Pentagon.

I was surrounded by intelligence, but the irony is that intelligence has never been one of my strengths. But to my advantage was an ability to verbally communicate biblical truth to highly intelligent people who thought I was intelligent. I had a lady in our church a number of years ago who said, "I know you're not, but you sound like you're smart."

I took that with two grains of salt.

What inspired me to write this book was a desire to try and set the record straight regarding some so-called "silly stories" in the Bible. You know, like Jonah and the whale, David and Goliath, Noah and the ark, and others. It seems like most people have been told the Bible was written by a bunch of primitive people sitting around a campfire, but there is a redemptive theme in the Scriptures that is beyond the ability for any human or AI to manufacture or dream up.

One day, I heard the comedian and TV host Bill Maher mocking the Scriptures on some news feed. I sensed God's Spirit saying, "Are you going to take that lying down?"

So, I went to my computer and started writing.

Keep this in mind: I like Bill Maher. I would not want to debate him. He is one very smart guy. But I like the fact that he's honest and that he points his rhetorical firepower at whomever he thinks needs it. He blasts Democrats and Republicans alike.

I believe what I have to say in the pages that follow will help three types of people: those who are genuine followers of Christ but have trouble defending their faith, those who are religious but don't understand that salvation is a gift and cannot be earned, and those who would call themselves atheists or agnostics. Most of the book is directed toward the latter.

I humbly enter into these treacherous waters. I do not want to come across haughty or arrogant, but with a teachable spirit. With eighty-one years under my belt, I feel I have earned the right to share my thoughts.

Contents

Introduction

Bill Maher is hands down my favorite agnostic/atheist. He is funny, sarcastic, really quick on his feet, and wicked smart. He never throws Christianity under the bus, though he likes to put it under a tractor mower with the blades running at full speed.

When Bill gives us an intellectual uppercut, we don't know what hit us. If you are in a debate, this is the guy you want in your foxhole—unless it has to do with the Bible.

A few weeks back, I saw a clip of Bill mocking the story of and the ark. It was really funny, and there was a woman beside him laughing hysterically. The humor was there for those who saw the forest but not the trees. From a flyover point of view, the whole story seems absurd, and rightly so. A gazillion animals climbing on this little boat, what could be funnier? However, for those of us who have entered the forest of the biblical narrative and examined the details of the roots, the bark, the limbs, and the leaves, a whole new world emerges.

I gave it some serious thought and decided I would write a book for Bill, his followers, and anyone who wishes to eavesdrop. This book is an attempt to set the record straight by pulling back the curtain on some of Bill's takes regarding the supposed foolishness of Scripture. In the pages that follow, I will have an imaginary conversation with Bill in his living room. Even though I'm addressing my comments toward Bill Maher, I am also using him as a representative of the agnostic or atheist worldview. It's hard to make this a two-way conversation, but I will try and reply to some of Bill's comments directly, as well as common ideas from people who do not believe in God.

I want to respond to Maher's sarcasm, which I must admit is the best in the business. Though Bill's humor can push the envelope, a smile creeps across my face as I put myself in the shoes of the unbeliever.

So I thought I might return the favor by responding to some of Bill's favorite Bible stories and unpacking them from a different point of view. I want to show Bill what I see in those stories that he doesn't. So I will pick some of his favorites. This is not to make Bill and his humanistic friends look foolish—that would be hard to do, since I'm not that clever, and many of them are much smarter than I am.

In order to move forward, I need to give some understanding as to how the Bible is meant to be interpreted for those who have never read it, and to remove some false understandings that you may have picked up by asking others who are equally ignorant. This is a very brief overview of what might be taught in a four-year seminary degree. I never went to seminary myself, but I have been reading and studying and teaching the Bible as a pastor for over fifty years.

Bill, people like yourself who don't know their Bible I want to teach you some theology as you teach others your world view of agnosticism. Once we both know where the other is coming from it will make dialogue much more profitable. Christians might learn a few things as well. Here we go.

What Is the Bible?

Bill, I'm certain you're aware of the "telephone" game, where twenty people gather in a living room and the first person says, "I love potato chips with mayonnaise." Everyone passes along what he thinks was said, until finally the last person hears, "My boss wants a raise." I heard a comedian recently mocking the Bible by saying it has been translated and re-translated over and over again, so what we have today are the last words spoken in the telephone game. The crowd was laughing hysterically. Yet that is not how the Bible came to be. If that were the case, the Bible would be an enormous word salad with no progressive narrative. However, it is exactly the opposite. It is the most finely tuned writing in the history of the world, incorporating poetry, parables, polemic, prose, and narrative, all telling one story that points to the Messiah, Jesus Christ.

The Bible has sixty-six books, thirty-nine in the Old Testament and twenty-seven in the New Testament. Those books were written over a *fifteen-hundred-year* period by some forty authors, most of whom never knew one another; yet they all tell the same story. Let that sink in. Isaiah never knew Moses, and David lived long before Daniel. Yet when one writer passed on, he metaphorically left his quill pen for the next man to continue the redemptive theme. This is known as the *Unfolding Drama of Redemption*. For you and your unbelieving tribe, Bill, this will be a whole new world. It might be new for many who are followers of Jesus as well.

But if we don't understand the purpose for which the Bible was written, then everything in it will appear foreign, out of place, on the wrong side of history, outdated, behind the times, and antiquated. The Bible itself tells us why it was written: "to make you wise for salvation through faith in Christ Jesus" (2 Tim. 3:15). More on this later. The Scriptures are not behind the times but infinitely ahead of the times, for Jesus is the Alpha and the Omega, the Beginning and the End. The Bible is not on the wrong side of history; it records history before it happens.

Another aspect that will help make the metanarrative of Scripture digestible is that the entire Bible, from beginning to end, is about Jesus. He will appear in the prophets, the psalms, and all the writings of the Old Testament. All types of genres are employed in the Old Testament to point to the One who was to come. There is poetry, polemics, narrative, and prose. It has been said that *the Old Testament is the New Testament concealed, and the New Testament is the Old Testament revealed.* This is known as the *unfolding drama of redemption.* No human being or group of human beings could have written something like this without the Spirit of God to guide them. In Scripture, the term *redemption* means to have our freedom bought and paid for. Left to our own devices, we are stuck as slaves to sin, and we owe the penalty due to our transgression—and the "wages of sin is death" (Rom. 6:23). Sin is simply any violation of God's law. It is rebellion against the will of God. But if we are slaves to sin, how can we find liberty? To redeem a slave is to pay for him to be taken off the slave market and be set free. For a person to be redeemed, he or she must accept the payment Christ made for their sin and stop trying to redeem themselves through good works. There is no picking yourself up by your own bootstraps. Ain't gonna happen. Jesus Christ paid the penalty we owed in order to redeem us from sin, death, and hell, and all we can do is accept it and believe.

Again, I'm not trying to give the reader a mini seminary class, but an understanding of how this is all put together. If we don't know where we are going, we will never arrive. But here's something else about Scripture the reader must know: When we read it, we are taken into the *world of the unknown*. God is not revealing to us the things we are capable of learning on our own. He doesn't tell us how to make a cake, but he does tell us how to enter the kingdom of God.

In the pages that follow, we will be on a journey, diving into some of the stories that cause people to question the sanity of the writer and the one who believes it. I would ask the doubter to head into this book with an open mind, which is often hard to do since we already have a parking space in our brain for bias. Some of us are double parked.

So, Bill, put on your seat belt and buckle up; this might be a bumpy ride. And just so you know, here is a word from Scripture to those who don't believe: "For the word of the cross is folly to those who are perishing, but to us who are being saved it is the power of God. For it is written, 'I will destroy the wisdom of the wise, and the discernment of the discerning I will thwart'" (1 Cor. 1:18–19). This is being played out daily. Now that we know where each other stands, we can start our conversation.

Chapter 1:

Bill's Favorite Bible Stories, and Their Underlying

Truth

Bill, I'm sure you know the old adage, you can't tell a book by its cover. When it comes to the Bible, you told Jordan Peterson that "it has these things that are comically stupid and corrupt."[1] What I hope to accomplish in this book is to reveal to you and those who think like you Bill, that what appears to be "comically stupid" is seriously true. So, I want to start by opening the book for you and taking some of your favorite Bible stories and unpacking them one at a time. But in order to set the stage, let's take a look at some of the silliest stories that anyone can observe with their own eyes. The great pyramid in Giza Egypt is beyond explanation. It has two and a half million stones, some weighing in at 468 tons. But here is the kicker, they were quarried 250 miles away. Sorry, but there were no aircraft carriers in those days and if there were we don't have the capacity to lift such a weight today according to The Guiness World Book of Records. Now just for a second, let your mind escape any bias. Suppose the bible described such a structure but there is no evidence that it ever existed. The heat, wind and sand erased any trace of such an architectural marvel. Any architect worth his salt wouldn't give such a theory the slightest bit of credibility or his license would be in jeopardy, much like a scientist who denies evolution. Many have lost their jobs.

Let's take this illustration a step further. Suppose the bible recorded the building of the Great Wall of China which stretches about

---

[1] Interview with Jordan Peterson, *Real Time with Bill Maher*, HBO, August 5, 2023.

13,000 miles across the most undulating terrain on the planet, yet without a trace of such a colossal marvel. Who would fall for such a ruse? My point is, that when the bible describes enormous fetes such as the building of the Ark it is laughable. So, let's open our eyes and step into another world.

"Silly" Story Number One: The Creation of the Universe

Let's start by taking a look at the universe and where it came from. According to the late pastor and theologian Dr. R. C. Sproul, there are four possible scenarios for how the universe came into being.[2]

1) The universe created itself.

2) The universe is an illusion.

3) The universe has always been.

4) God created the universe

I think logic can remove the first two. The most popular view, though highly debated regarding the details, is the Big Bang theory, which tells us that the universe at one time was a point of singularity. In other words, all the matter that exists today was once the size of a golf ball. Though that golf ball has always existed and no one knows where it came from, for some reason it exploded at four o'clock one Thursday afternoon. Every high school sophomore should recognize the flaw in the physics here. It was the great Sir Isaac Newton who said that an object at rest will remain at rest unless acted upon by an outside object, and every object in motion will remain in motion unless acted upon by an outside object. So, what was the outside object that made the Big Bang to explode into stars and galaxies and planets? It would have to have movement, power, and intelligence to pull this off. It would have to be a living being. That being could

---

[2] R. C. Sproul, *Does God Exist?* (Ligonier, 2019), 9–10.

only be God, and He holds all men accountable for believing in His existence. "For his invisible attributes, namely, his eternal power and divine nature, have been clearly perceived, ever since the creation of the world, in the things that have been made. So, they are without excuse" (Rom. 1:20).

Bill, let's examine the biblical view of how everything came to be. I suspect you can quote the first verse of the Bible: "In the beginning, God created the heavens and the earth" (Gen. 1:1). When a story starts out this way, you know it is not meant to be a fable, but a historical and factual account. It is "in the beginning," not "once upon a time." But let's consider this opening verse, which explained to ancient people—and explains to all people for all time—how the world came into being. Keep in mind that the Bible's words were written by primitive people who had no access to a microscope, telescope, or the Hubble Telescope.

In the beginning: **That's time.**

God created: **That's energy.**

The heavens: **That's space.**

The Earth: **That's matter.**

The Encyclopedia Britannica says, "The universe is everything that exists, including objects and energy, throughout time and space."[3] The opening sentence of the Bible is saying the same thing, even though it was written thirty-five-hundred years ago. What a lucky guess!

Bill, my friend, I know what you want to say. *What a stretch!* But pause for a moment and ask yourself, what is the probability the opening line of the Bible would contain the truth of what all science

---

[3] "universe" in *Britannica Kids*, accessed February 17, 2025, http://kids.britannica.com/kids/article/universe/400293.

has discovered over millennia? Zero! It might well have opened with, "Once upon a time, there was a big man in the sky with a long white beard and when he laughed the world fell out of his belly."

Keep in mind, Bill, that Moses, who wrote the words of Genesis, was well-educated for his time, but he had none of our modern knowledge of science or the universe. Yet he nailed what the universe is made of in one brief statement.

Try as you may, there is no escaping this truth. It appears there may be a mastermind behind this opening verse who knew an awful lot about creation. Such knowledge hints at the reality of a creator.

"Silly" Story Number Two: The Origin of Life

Both theists and non-theists wrestle with three big questions regarding life: Where did we come from? Why are we here? And where are we going when we die? Each person is confronted with these big three. The atheist says that life has evolved, that there is no purpose in life, and that when we die, we become fine dining for worms at their favorite subterranean restaurant.

In the materialistic worldview, millions of years ago lightning struck ooze in the Nile River, and voila, a cell was formed with the ability to replicate itself. Bill, you and your followers say you don't believe in miracles, yet the formation of the cell—arguably the most complex basic structure for all life forms—makes the parting of the Red Sea look like child's play.

While we are at it, let's open up another can of worms— evolution. No matter how much you might think the science is "settled," neither you nor I can prove our positions employing the scientific method, which demands that any hypothesis must go through the rigorous screening process of what is observable, reproducible, and measurable. No one has observed life spontaneously emerging from non-life, and neither has anyone observed God forming dirt into the shape of a man and breathing the breath of life into Him.

Therefore, creationists and evolutionists do not ultimately have a scientific leg to stand on. For me, Bill, I couldn't believe in evolution even if I didn't believe in the God of the Bible. One of my favorite unwitting defenders of creation is an atheist named David Attenborough. Many of us have seen his work on the BBC as he travels the world over, filming the most incredible displays of every kind of creature—from spiders with the most complex webs to fish that have unique compensating lenses that correct for the bending of light when it strikes water. This fish spits water to knock bugs off of low-hanging branches, but without the corrective lens, it would miss every time. So here is the big question: How many eons did it take for the spider and the fish to develop such survival skills? "Early" models would have died off within days, and that would have been the end of that species. This is true of all living creatures.

The reason so many people believe in evolution is that they have been indoctrinated in it through school, with the supposed proof being the fossil record. The media has assisted, convincing the public that the fossil record reveals a smooth-running story without any gaps. The problem is that the media knows nothing about fossils and couldn't find a flawed argument if they tried. But the scientific world has the upper hand and encourages this one-sided perspective. A number of years ago, archeologists found what looked like the nail in the coffin for creationists, but it was later found to be a hoax. You had to look really hard to find a retraction. Google the "Piltdown man" for all the details.

Who is going to listen to a scientific argument from the church? What do we know? For the last twenty years, mathematicians have been challenging biologists on the probability of evolution, which seems to be basically zero. There was simply not enough time for life to develop on its own. And no amount of time would be enough for that to occur. Many in the scientific community have jumped ship on this philosophy. However, what is observable, reproducible and measurable is what scripture says about man.

"He (Jesus) went on: What comes out of a person of a person is what defiles them. For it is from within, out of a person's heart, that evil thoughts come-sexual immorality, theft, murder, adultery, greed, malice, deceit, lewdness, envy, slander, arrogance and folly. All these evils come from inside and defile a person" (Matt. 15:11-20). This you can count on every day. We live it out moment by moment, but we don't like what Jesus says. It's certainly not flattering. But we know it's true. Here is something that is readily observable.

However, when it comes to evolution, we swallow it hook, line, and sinker? To offer creation as an option would be to capitulate to the Bible, which is frowned upon in the public square. To shoot down any biblical discussion, phrases get tossed around such as *science says, the data proves, statistics reveal,* and *studies show.* But a careful peek under the hood tells another story. Believe me, I am a big fan of science. I wouldn't be alive if it weren't for science. But I'm talking about true science. Bogus science uses intimidation. True science puts the facts on the table and avoids statements like, "We think that perhaps maybe twenty million years ago a fox could have turned into a whale."

Evolution couldn't be more unscientific. Which is why it is slowly and surely decaying under the watchful eye of true science. But what is the alternative? To believe in what the Bible says about creation? We certainly can't lower ourselves to such foolishness.

Here is another interesting phenomenon: When they get stuck, our scientific community often falls back on the "alien explanation." How could the Egyptians have built the pyramids without the aid of power tools, dynamite, and massive bulldozers? Aliens to the rescue.

Aliens are now the ones who built the pyramids. Certainly not everyone believes this, but over half the nation believes in life on other planets. Why? If evolution is ever determined to be totally implausible, and I think we're knocking on that door, why would we think there is life elsewhere? We keep pushing the problem back to outer space. We love the thought of other creatures out there. We want to believe it. When you want something to be true, you will look for evidence to confirm it, and if you look hard enough, rest assured you will find it.

Let's move farther out into the universe. Because there are billions of stars, planets, and galaxies, we employ the mathematics of probability. Surely, there must be life given such astronomical numbers. Add time and chance to the equation, and life suddenly appears. Not so fast. We are pitting probability against possibility. Is it possible that life was started by lightning striking ooze on planet X? I have tried to show that evolution is impossible here, so why would it be likely there? Given enough time and chance, along with endless galaxies, could there be a place where two plus two equals five? Chance has no inherent power. It does not have a brain. It is merely a filler when there is no scientific explanation.

Truth doesn't change, no matter how far out we go. Our astronauts use the same math, science, and logic out in space as they do here on earth. When you put all this together, there is only one logical choice, which is that the God of this universe is fully in charge and is the Creator of all things and needs no help from us trying to explain Him away. Strangely, atheists do not believe in miracles, yet they believe that life came from non-life. But when believers refer to the non-life of Jesus in the grave and then rising from the grave to life, they balk at the concept.

"Silly" Story Number Three: The Snake

"On your belly you shall go, and dust you shall eat all the days of your life" (Gen. 3:14). Hey, Bill, do you know why snakes flick their tongues? This is from LIVE Science:

> When a snake flicks its tongue, it collects odors that are present in miniscule moisture particles floating through the air. The snake darts its tongue into its Jacobson's organ, which is located inside the roof of the snake's mouth.[4]

Those particles are dust. Just as God said. Pretty cool, huh? Not bad for ancient primitive people—unless there was a divine inspiration behind it. Suppose it had said that a snake would eat cockroaches all the days of his life? We could prove this to be wrong in a minute.

"Silly" Story Number Four: Noah and the Ark

Bill, I think this one is your favorite. It is certainly a prime target for mockery. This little boat carrying all the wildlife of the world has got to be the height of incredulity. Come on, man. But let's see what we can see discover from what is revealed in Scripture and from what we know about buoyancy. The ark was not designed as a speedboat or Carnival Cruise Line. It was built like a barge.

Let's look at the ark's dimensions through the lens of Henry Morris, who once headed up the civil engineering dept of the Virginia Polytechnic Institute. He says, "The question is: how long

---

[4] Remy Melina, "Why Does a Snake Flick Its Tongue?," *Live Science*, June 6, 2011, https://www.livescience.com/33325-snake-flick-tongue.html.

is a cubit? . . . Most believe the biblical cubit to be 18 inches."[5] Morris goes on to give us more information with his calculations as a mathematician. "With the dimensions as calculated, the total volumetric capacity of the Ark was approximately 1,400,000 cubic feet, which is equal to the volumetric capacity of 522 standard livestock cars such as used on modern American railroads. Since it is known that about 240 sheep can be transported in one stock car, a total of over 125,000 sheep could have been carried in the Ark."

Though we don't have all the answers for every question, it remains amazing that there were no mistakes made regarding the dimensions of the ark. It could have been portrayed as twenty feet wide and a hundred feet high, which would have caused it to capsize upon launching. Keep in mind, no one had built such a vessel before, and Noah needed a divine blueprint. The ark has almost the exact

dimensions as the *Queen Mary* in her day. How could such primitive people know such things about buoyancy and ship hydrostatics? If the dimensions recorded were off by the slightest degree, we would toss out the Scriptures as not being inspired. The guesswork of such uneducated people regarding how to build such a sturdy, seaworthy vessel has such a low probability that to neglect such revelation is turning a blind eye to the truth. Keep in mind you don't need 250 dog kinds but two dogs that have the genetic pool to create 250 dog kinds. This is true of the other animals.

"Silly" Story Number Five: Jonah

This is probably the number one book in Scripture that is seen by secular humanists as being, well, a little fishy. (Sorry, I couldn't help it.) It is beyond credulity. This is the place to hit the proverbial

---

[5] Henry Morris, *The Genesis Record: A Scientific and Devotional Commentary on the Book of Beginnings* (Baker Book House, 1976), 181.

punching bag. How could any sane person believe such nonsense? A man being swallowed by a great fish? Christianity and Judaism rise and fall on this book. If we can sink Jonah, pun intended, we can sink the Bible. Since I will come back to this story under another heading, I won't go too far at this point, other than to mention that right in the middle of Jonah's short four-chapter book we read, "To the roots of the mountains I sank down" (Jonah 2:6). I'm quite curious how Jonah knew there were mountains at the bottom of the ocean? Jacques Cousteau had not yet arrived on the scene. Bill, when do you think man first discovered there were mountains at the bottom of the ocean? Are you ready for this? It has been just a little over seventy years.

So many lucky guesses about the universe, snake's appetites, perfect dimensions for a boat to be seaworthy, and now mountains at the bottom of the sea. What are the odds? Either that is a whole lot of luck, or we have to admit that all this is quite amazing and has no human explanation.

"Silly" Story Number Six: Israel

"Now the LORD said to Abram, 'Go from your country and your kindred and your father's house to the land that I will show you. And I will make of you a great nation, and I will bless you and make your name great, so that you will be a blessing. I will bless those who bless you, and him who dishonors you I will curse, and in you all the families of the earth shall be blessed'" (Gen. 12:1–3).

Let's go back to the issue of probability. God made a covenant with Abram, who would later be called Abraham. God told him that the Jewish people would bless the world. Today, approximately .02 percent of the world's population is Jewish, yet about 20 percent of Nobel Prize winners have been Jewish. What is the probability that the Bible would make such a bold prediction, knowing the probability of this coming to pass is close to zero? Had Israel failed as a nation and been wiped off the map, the Bible would be just another book that failed in its guesses about the future.

Here are some questions for you, Bill: Where did the nation of Israel come from? Were Adam and Eve fictitious? What about Cain and Abel? What about Noah? What about his three sons, Shem, Ham, and Japheth? What about Shem, through whom Abraham would come? Was Abraham an invented character? What about Isaac, Jacob, and Joseph? Was the pharaoh a made-up king? What about the twelve sons of Jacob settling in Egypt, where the nation of Israel started? Was that just a story? Is Israel a present-day nation? Is that a fictitious story? Where do we draw the line between fact and fiction? The nation of Israel is a miracle, and I don't use the word casually.

Bill, let me take you through a brief history as to how the nation of Israel came to be. As I trace the storyline, see if you can determine where the supposed fable ends and real history begins. Perhaps you have heard of Joseph and the coat of many colors given to him by his father, Jacob. It is one of the most fascinating stories in all literature. The narrative goes from Genesis 37 to 50.

The three main patriarchs in the Old Testament were Abraham, Isaac, and Jacob. Jacob was a scoundrel and a cheat, but God uses all kinds of people to bring forth His story of redemption. Jacob favored his youngest son, Joseph, and made him a coat of many colors. That did not sit well with Joseph's brothers, who became enraged with jealousy. To make matters worse, Joseph shared a dream he had in which his brothers were all bowing down to him. Their hatred grew stronger by the day.

One day, Jacob sent Joseph on a mission to see how his brothers were getting along in tending Jacob's flock in a place called Shechem. When Joseph arrived in Shechem, his brothers were not there. However, there was a man who noticed Joseph wandering around in a field. He said to Joseph, "What are you seeking?" (Gen. 37:15). Joseph said he was looking for his brothers. The man said, "I heard them say, 'Let us go to Dothan'" (Gen. 37:17).

Let me interrupt here and make an observation. If that man had not overheard the brothers say they were going to Dothan, the nation of Israel would not exist today. This little detail of a man who "happened" to be there to point Joseph toward his brothers is one of thousands of such "coincidences" that God reveals in the Bible to show how He brought all His plans to pass.

Anyway, as Joseph got closer to where his brothers were, they spotted him and said, "Come now, let's kill him and throw him into one of these cisterns and say that a ferocious animal devoured him. Then we'll see what comes of his dreams" (Gen. 37:20).

So Joseph's brothers stripped him of his coat and dipped it in the blood of a goat in order to make it look like he had been killed by a wild animal. They showed it to their father Jacob to make him suffer, since he had shown favoritism to Joseph. Jealousy can lead people to such hatred they are willing to kill.

As Joseph lay in the pit, a traveling band of traders came by, and his brothers sold him into slavery. Joseph ended up in the house of Potiphar, a high-ranking official in Pharaoh's government. Joseph's life was so above reproach that Potiphar put Joseph in charge of his house and all he had. However, Potiphar's wife had eyes for Joseph, and she tried to seduce him day after day. One day, she attacked him, and he fled, leaving his cloak in her hand. She told the servants and her husband that Joseph had tried to rape her. Joseph was subsequently thrown into prison.

Had he not been thrown into prison, Israel would not exist today. The details of this narrative are without gaps. While in prison, there were two other prisoners, a butler and a baker who had previously worked for Pharaoh. Both had dreams that troubled them. Joseph said, "Do not interpretations belong to God? Tell me your dreams" (Gen. 40:8). Now, follow this carefully.

Joseph told the butler that his dream meant that he would be getting out of prison and going back to work for Pharaoh, while he revealed that the baker was going to lose his head. Both dreams came true. When the butler got out, Joseph told him, "Don't forget me," but the butler forgot him. Now, here is an interesting twist in the story. Had Joseph been released right away, Israel would not exist today. You see, Pharaoh had a dream two years after Joseph's encounter with the butler. The king was troubled because no one in his court could interpret the dream. The butler remembered—better late than never—that he met a man in prison who could interpret dreams. Pharaoh said, "Go get that man." Joseph was released and stood before the most powerful man in the world, who told Joseph his dream. Pharaoh was so impressed that he recognized the Spirit of God in Joseph's life and made Joseph second in command of all of Egypt.

The dream of Pharaoh was that Egypt would have seven years of plenty and seven years of famine. Joseph said Egypt needed to store up the grain so when the famine hit, they would have food and be able to sell to other nations. Guess who came down to buy grain during the famine? That's right—Joseph's brothers. Joseph's own dream came true as his brothers bowed down to him. Joseph knew who they were, but they had no idea who he was.

Joseph devised a plan to find out if they had true remorse for what they had done to him. He eventually revealed himself and assured them they need not fear him. Though Joseph could have had them executed in an act of revenge, forgiveness led the way. He told his brothers to go back to the land of Canaan and get their father to move to Goshen, which was a rich piece of land in northern Egypt. They did so, and the twelve tribes of Israel were formed there. No gaps, just reality. There is much more to that story, Bill, so I encourage you to read the whole dramatic narrative!

Like everything else in the Bible, the Joseph story is part of a continuous flow recorded by many different authors who never knew one another yet continued the same theme and pointed to the coming Messiah.

God had to have a nation through whom the Messiah would come. He chose Abraham to be the father of that great nation. Why didn't God pick a big, powerful nation that no other nation would mess with? God had predicted that this little nation would stand the test. Has it? Is this a miracle? Is it still standing, though much bigger and more powerful nations have come and gone? How could this be? Like the all-encompassing scientific explanation of how the universe began and the scientific understanding of how snakes collect dust particles and the perfect dimensions of the ark, and Jonah discovering mountains at the bottom of the ocean, so has God has brought forth the nation of Israel.

"Silly" Story Number Seven: David and Goliath

Here we have another absurd narrative about a runt teenager, David, defeating an experienced warrior, Goliath. However, I must dive into a little background so there is some context in which to navigate. You will notice, Bill, that taking Bible stories out of their context gives the skeptic a great deal of leverage to make any biblical account look childish. I have shown the redemptive theme in all these so-called silly stories. This one is mindboggling. Put on your thinking cap as we are going to take a deep dive into the text.

The story of David and Goliath is found in 1 Samuel 17. King Saul had gathered the Israelite troops on a hill on one side of a valley, while the Philistines assembled on the other side. No rivalry in the NFL could match this because of what hung in the balance. The entire world was at stake regarding who won that battle. It would prove to be the greatest battle the world has ever known. How can I make such a statement? Because the future of Israel and the coming of the Messiah was on the line. Whoever won this battle would be slaves to their enemy.

Let's find out where all this began. As with everything in Scripture, it began in Genesis. As Adam fell, sin entered the world. God declared war on Satan with these words: "And I will put enmity between you and the woman, and between your offspring and hers; he will crush your head, and you will strike his heel" (Gen. 3:15 NIV).

This is considered the first mention of the gospel in the Bible. Here we have a prophetic statement about the offspring of the woman giving a death blow to the serpent and the serpent giving a temporary wound to the offspring of the woman. We could spend a whole book talking about this one verse, but, in short, it is pointing to the fact that Satan gave a temporary wound to Christ (the seed of the woman) at the crucifixion, but Christ crushed the head of Satan when He rose from the grave in glorious victory.

Going back to David and Goliath, this is not a story about a valiant young man we are supposed to emulate (contrary to popular interpretations). "Be strong and courageous like David," we are told. No, the point is that this young warrior foreshadows a greater "David" who steps in and wins battles on our behalf. Notice that the Israelites did nothing to earn the spoils of victory. David did everything for their salvation, just as Christ did everything for the salvation of those who believe and follow Him. We contribute nothing. What is revealed from one end of the Bible to the other is God's *gift* of salvation, but man's pride insists that his own good life will get him past the pearly gates. Not going to happen. Something else to keep in mind is that most of these authors contribute to this redemptive theme having never known one another. Remember the statement in Genesis 3:15, that the offspring of the woman would "crush" the head of the enemy? That is exactly what David did to Goliath. This was no silly story, but it was a picture of how Jesus would forever defeat Satan.

"Silly" Story Number Eight: Abraham and Isaac

We noted earlier how God called Abraham to be the father of the nation of Israel and the Jewish people. What we didn't mention was that Abraham was ninety years old at the time, and he had no children. It's hard to be the father of a nation when you're not a father at all! But through miraculous intervention, God gave a son named Isaac to Abraham and his aged wife, Sarah. But later in Isaac's life, we find one of the most troubling accounts in all the Bible.

In Genesis 22, God told Abraham to "take your son, your only son Isaac, whom you love, and go to the land of Moriah, and offer him there as a burnt offering on one of the mountains of which I shall tell you" (v. 2). Bill, doesn't it seem like God is contradicting Himself? On the one hand, He has raised up the promised son, Isaac, through whom the Messiah would come, but then He tells Abraham to offer up his son.

We note in verse 5, however, that Abraham told his servants to "stay here with the donkey while I and the boy go over there. We will worship and then we will come back to you." How can they return if Isaac is dead? In the New Testament, in Hebrews 11:17–19, we read that Abraham believed God could raise his son from the dead. And figuratively, that is what happened. As Abraham told Isaac, "God will provide for himself the lamb for a burnt offering." He did that literally, stopping Abraham from killing his son and providing an animal to be sacrificed in his place. But what is really going on is the anticipation of the cross and the resurrection of Jesus, two thousand years in advance. At the cross, the "Lamb of God" was sacrificed in the place of all of the unworthy sinners who deserved that penalty.

You see, Bill, stories that seem stupid and silly actually carry megatons of theological weight all connected to the unfolding drama of redemption.

"Silly" Story Number Nine: The Virgin Birth

Bill, the virgin birth of Jesus might be number one when it comes to that which seems incredulous in the pages of the Bible. But here again, it fits the redemption narrative and helps bring to completion the entire biblical narrative. This issue is complex, so we will ride on the surface and avoid theological jargon. The man Jesus had no human father, but He did have a human mother. Both are generally needed to create another human being, of course, but the line of sin needed to be interrupted. Even though Mary did come through the line of Adam, it would require a human father to carry on the sin line from Adam. The Holy Spirit planted the divine seed in Mary's womb so that Christ could be fully man and fully God. If this did not take place, then the sin of Adam would have been placed to the account of Christ, making Him a sinful creature. If you look at this in theological terms, it is more than apparent that this is no fable, but a carefully designed plan to save man from the penalty of sin.

"Silly" Story Number Ten: The Lion and the Lamb

Bill, here we find another interesting subject that initially seems irrelevant as we go through the Scriptures. But there is nothing irrelevant in the Bible. There are so many themes and subliminal themes that run from Genesis to Revelation. The subject of the lion and the lamb portrays the two natures of Jesus. He is the Lion from the tribe of Judah who will come again as the conquering King (Rev. 5:5), but He is also the Lamb of God who takes away the sin of the world (John 1:29). On the surface, this might seem to be another silly story, when it is one of the most powerful dimensions of the redemptive theme. These dueling metaphors of a lion and a lamb are book ends showing both immense weakness and immense strength.

21

We have to pause and put the pieces together. When Adam and Eve sinned, God immediately clothed them with the skins of an animal (Gen. 3:21). This is called *atonement*. Their sins were covered after the killing of an animal because "without the shedding of blood there is no forgiveness of sins" (Heb. 9:22).

The book of Leviticus tells us, "For the life of the flesh is in the blood, and I have given it for you on the altar to make atonement for your souls, for it is the blood that makes atonement by the life" (Lev.17:11). You might note, Bill, that it does not say your eye makes an atonement, or your ear, but the blood. When you go to the doctor to find out what is wrong, they don't run tests on your earwax or flaky skin, but on your blood. God, as the Creator of all life, is well aware that life is found in the blood. So here is a brief picture the lamb plays in Scripture.

Scripture moves from sacrificing one lamb for one man to sacrificing one lamb for a family at the Passover (Ex. 12:3–13). Then, once a year on the Day of Atonement, the high priest would go into the Holy of Holies in the tabernacle or temple to atone for the sins of the people (Lev. 16:1–5). Then, in the gospel of John, we read these words from John the Baptist. Speaking of Jesus, he says, "Behold the lamb of God, who takes away the sin of the world!" (John 1:29).

One lamb for one man, one lamb for a family, one lamb for a nation, and one Lamb for the world. You can't make this up. It is the unfolding drama of redemption stemming from Genesis 3:15, where God declares war on Satan, and one of the main players is a lamb, the Lamb.

And what about the Lion? The lion is the king of the jungle and is known to be an animal with great power. There are other powerful animals, but none symbolizes such strength as does the lion. He is a universal symbol of a conquering king. Jesus is the King of kings and the Conqueror of conquerors.

"Silly" Story Number Eleven: The Tower of Babel

Now the whole earth had one language and the same words. And as people migrated from the east, they found a plain in the land of Shinar and settled there. And they said to one another, "Come, let us make bricks, and burn them thoroughly." And they had brick for stone, and bitumen for mortar. Then they said, "Come, let us build ourselves a city and a tower with its top in the heavens, and let us make a name for ourselves, lest we be dispersed over the face of the whole earth." And the Lord came down to see the city and the tower, which the children of man had built. And the Lord said, "Behold, they are one people, and they have all one language, and this is only the beginning of what they will do. And nothing that they propose to do will now be impossible for them. Come, let us go down and there confuse their language, so that they may not understand one another's speech." So the Lord dispersed them from there over the face of all the earth, and they left off building the city. Therefore its name was called Babel, because there the Lord confused the language of all the earth. And from there the Lord dispersed them over the face of all the earth. (Gen. 11:1–9)

Here we have a very simple story that does not have any obvious purpose. Where all the languages came from is highly debatable. The point of this account is not to give out that information. There is a much bigger story here.

Theologians refer to the *first mention principle*. This principle says that whenever a subject is first mentioned in the Bible, it is usually the key to understanding the mind of God on that subject. In other words, the subject will stick its head up many times from one end of Scripture to the other.

The term *Babel* is very nuanced and can mean confusion or rapid, incomprehensible speech. But throughout Scripture the word *Babylon* speaks of rebellion toward God and is mentioned 280 times from Genesis to Revelation. So, as you can see, this city represents more than a place, but also man's rebellion toward God. To use modern terms, this would be the first mention of *secularism humanism*, in which man wants no part of God ruling over him. In the narrative there is no mention of God in their plans. They desire to go up, while God plans on coming down.

As I have mentioned, Bill, there are seemingly endless layers of themes in Scripture. This present world is Babylon on steroids. We just can't fix it. Every nation on the planet is living in fear of other nations. There was an old Coke ad with a beautiful tune and happy lyrics, which said, "I'd like to teach the world to sing in perfect harmony." I would, too, but as long as Babylon rules that will never happen.

Chapter 2:

Tackling Typology

Bill, I want to introduce you to a term that might be new to you, and that even many Christians are unfamiliar with: *typology*. I once heard a "type" defined any person, place, object, ceremony, event, or institution divinely adopted to represent some spiritual reality, or to prefigure the person of Christ, later to be revealed in the New Testament.

Let's take a look at a few examples of how types in the Old Testament point to the person and work of Jesus.

Joseph

Joseph was sold by his brothers for twenty pieces of silver (Gen. 37:28), while Jesus was sold for thirty pieces of silver (Matt: 26:15).

Joseph was innocent yet suffered greatly, just as Jesus was innocent and suffered greatly.

Joseph was sent by his father to look for his brothers, as Jesus was sent by His Father to look for the lost.

This goes on for a long time, but you get the idea.

Jonah

Jonah was a Jew. Jesus was a Jew.

Jonah was a male. Jesus was a male.

Jonah was asleep on a ship (Jonah 1:5). Jesus was asleep on a boat (Mark 4:38).

Jonah had to be awakened on the ship during a storm. Jesus was awakened on the boat during a storm.

Jonah told the sailors that he must die so others can live. "Pick me up and hurl me into the sea; then the sea will quiet down for you" (Jonah 1:12). Jesus said He would give His life as a ransom for many (Mark 10:45). He willingly died so others might live.

Jonah was three days and three nights in the belly of the great fish, as Jesus was three days and three nights in the heart of the earth (Matt. 12:40).

There is simply no way to brush this off by saying this was a self-fulfilled prophecy. There comes a time in every heart where bias must be laid to rest. The evidence is overwhelming that God is sovereign over all of human history, even when He uses stories that appear to be foolish. A more careful examination reveals a deeper truth. "He who has ears to hear, let him hear" (Matt. 11:15).

The men on board the ship ignored Jonah and tried to save themselves by rowing to shore, *but they could not* (Jonah 1:13). Bill, this is a message to all religious people who are trying to earn their salvation by impressing God with good works. *But they could not.* Salvation is a gift and must be received as such. Any attempt to earn salvation by doing good things will be met with that reality: *but they could not.* Even the subject of salvation is revealed through typology. Amazing!

Jonah later said, "Salvation belongs to the LORD!" (2:9). He did not say that salvation is from leading a good life.

Noah's Ark

Jesus claims to be the only way to come to the Father and escape judgment. The ark built by Noah was the only way to avoid judgment from the great flood, since it is recorded that man was evil beyond measure. The Scriptures tell us, "Every intention of the thoughts of his heart was only evil continually" (Gen. 6:5). Thus, the ark is a type of Christ. Another interesting fact is revealed: "So make

26

yourself an ark of cypress wood; make rooms in it and coat it with pitch inside and out" (Gen. 6:14). Note the details of making sure there were no leaks, but even more fascinating is the Hebrew word for pitch is *kophar*. It means a covering or atonement. You just can't make these things up. Jesus is our true covering. So let's put this together as recorded. What kind of a fable chronicles the details for the nautical specifications of a large seaworthy vessel so it won't capsize? What kind of fable covers the details of sealing the vessel when the people at that time had never seen a flood. What kind of a fable would make up a story the represents a future Savior?

Here is something very intriguing. I have recorded the dimensions of the ark as revealed in Scripture. God gives us the length, width, and height of the ark. Nautical engineers have It also gives us the dimensions of the window above, but no dimensions of the door. Why leave out that one? Because if there were dimensions to the door, it would indicate limitations for entrance. Jesus said this in John 10:9: "I am the door. If anyone enters by me, he will be saved and will go in and out and find pasture." Note the word *anyone*. No restrictions.

The Passover

The two greatest events in the Old Testament are the parting of the Red Sea and the Passover. Let me put the latter event in context, which will help give it some relevance. Moses had gone to Pharoah and told the king that God demanded, "Let my people go" (e.g., Ex. 5:1). This request led to a long battle between Pharoah and the people of Israel. Moses became a savior as he battled the satanic forces of Egypt, thus becoming a type of Christ. Ten plagues were leveled against Pharoah, which were blood, frogs, lice, flies, livestock boils, hail, locust, darkness, and death. Why was death last? Because, the Bible says, "the last enemy to be destroyed is death" (1 Cor. 15:26). God referred to Israel as His "firstborn son" (Ex. 4:22). If

Pharoah was to kill the Lord's firstborn, then Pharoah would pay in kind. The people of Israel were instructed by the Lord to slay a lamb and sprinkle its blood over the doorpost and along the sides. On the night of Passover, the Lord would see the blood on the homes of the Jews and Passover. The doors of the Egyptians were not covered, and thus their the firstborn sons would be struck down. The blood of the lamb protected the Israelites. Note carefully the instructions given about the Passover lamb: "It shall be eaten in one house; you shall not take any of the flesh outside the house, and you shall not break any of its bones. All the congregation of Israel shall keep it" (Ex. 12:46–47).

Now let's jump to the New Testament and the crucifixion of Jesus Christ. Read these words ever so carefully: "Since it was the day of Preparation, and so that the bodies would not remain on the cross on the Sabbath (for that Sabbath was a high day), the Jews asked Pilate that their legs might be broken and that they might be taken away. So the soldiers came and broke the legs of the first, and of the other who had been crucified with him. But when they came to Jesus and saw that he was already dead, they did not break his legs" (John 19:31–33).

Tell me how you pull off the precision of such foreshadowing and fulfillment. Impossible. Then to make it even more clear, we read in 1 Corinthians 5:7 that "Christ, our Passover lamb, has been sacrificed."

You see, Bill, there is a great deal of typology that simply can't be forged in the annals of fables and wild speculation.

Bill, the purpose of this book is not to try and defend the existence of God. He needs no defense. My objective is for you to see another side of God's divine revelation by allowing you to look behind the curtain and see the Scriptures from a different angle. It is to let you know that Bible-believing people from Isaac Newton,

Werner Von Braun, Galileo, Copernicus, Kepler, and many others were no fools. Newton, arguably one of the smartest men to ever live, believed in God. His brain was the size of Jupiter.

Time does not permit us to go through every story in the Bible that you and others mock, but I wanted to give you a glimpse of the divine reality of His revelation that cannot be ignored nor denied. I am trying to hit the main areas of your objections.

Bill, I have often said to my congregation that when we open the Bible, we are entering the world of the unknown. We can only know with our five human senses. However, the Bible gives believers a sixth sense. Scripture says, "For the word of the cross is folly to those who are perishing, but to us who are being saved it is the power of God" (1 Cor. 1:18).

You see Bill, when the world rejects the ways of God, we reap what we sow. Have you seen the news lately? "He catches the wise in their craftiness" (1 Cor. 3:19). What this means is similar to teaching our children how to ride a bike. "Let me steady you, Timmy, as I keep one hand on the bike." "No!" yells the child. "I can do it myself." Dad lets go, and down goes Timmy. This is a very simplified version of what it looks like for God to take man in his own wisdom as man rejects the wisdom of God.

To use another picture, it's like quicksand. The harder we fight to get out, the more God rejects us, and the faster down we go. In the book of Romans, the first chapter spells out all we will ever need to know about why this world is a disaster, heading nowhere faster and faster through mind-blowing technology and human wisdom, which is no wisdom at all.

Chapter 3:

Vacationing in Utopia

"How was the beach?"

"It was a dream come true. A literal utopia."

We tend to think of our favorite vacation spot as utopia. Mankind is always looking for utopia, but in the long haul, he never finds it. The dream world turns into a nightmare. There are too many roadblocks that keep utopia at bay. Broken relationships, loss of health, rebellious children, broken marriages, or disillusioning new jobs. We keep looking for utopia, but it's always just over the horizon the way the pot of gold is at the end of the rainbow. Chase it forever, and it will always be just out of reach. Utopia is, in fact, a mirage. We will talk more about the mirage on in chapter 5. C. S. Lewis once said, "If I find in myself a desire which no experience in this world can satisfy, the most probable explanation is that I was made for another world."[6] Strangely, the Bible records the great desire of Abraham regarding this same quest for another world. "He was looking forward to the city that has foundations, whose designer and builder is God" (Heb. 11:10).

Bill, here are some reasons that utopia can't be found in this present world. The first one seems a bit juvenile at first blush, but I would tattoo this on the back of my eyelids: *Wherever you go, you're going to be there.* We all have problems. We all have mental baggage that we put in the overhead compartment of our minds. We all have a mental parking space for worry. (Some are double parked.) So,

---

[6] C. S. Lewis, *Mere Christianity* (HarperCollins, 2000), 136–137.

when we go to Disney or on a cruise, *we* will be there with all our worries and guilt. Vacations are just a temporary relief from the daily stress of life.

Just look at past history. Has any nation found the secret? We keep looking for it, through technical advancements and medical research, which are often helpful but never scratch that eternal itch. There are countless self-help books on the market. But "self" is the last place we will find help. Remember this: *We are the problem, and when the problem tries to solve the problem, that's a problem.*

Bill, I know you think the Bible is foolish and lacks any real credibility. So let's take a look at the world in which we live and how Scripture has anticipated this. No one denies the fact that mankind is increasing in knowledge at an exponential rate. We are doubling our knowledge in some areas every year. The computer industry cannot keep up with itself. And now we have AI knocking on the door. But there is a fly in the ointment (Eccl. 10:1). Knowledge is designed to solve problems, but simple observation shows that problems are increasing as fast as knowledge increases. This is what I call *the ultimate contradiction.* It makes no sense at all.

The following words were delivered by the Secretary General of the United Nations U Thant in the early 1970s before twenty-five hundred people, including statesmen and scholars from around the world:

> What element is lacking so that with all **our** skill and all **our** knowledge, we still find ourselves in the dark valley of discord and enmity? What is it that inhibits us from going forward together to enjoy the fruits of **human** endeavor and to reap the harvest of **human** experience? Why is it that, for all **our** professed ideals, **our** hopes, and **our** skills, peace on earth is still

a distant objective seen only dimly through the storms and turmoil of our present difficulties?[7]

Mr. Thant was echoing my very point. He talked about all our knowledge, skills, hopes, and ideals, which seem futile even in the midst of increased knowledge. How can this be? Here is another prescient quote, this time from the apostle Paul:

> But understand that in the last days, there will come times of difficulty. For people will be lovers of self, lovers of money, proud, arrogant, abusive, disobedient to their parents, ungrateful, unholy, heartless, unappeasable, slanderous, without self-control, brutal, not loving good, treacherous, reckless, swollen with conceit, lovers of pleasure rather than lovers of God. (2 Tim. 3:1–4)

Now if there were ever a more foolish statement, I don't know what it would be. Why would Paul stick his neck out and risk his reputation by declaring that the future would only get worse? Didn't he know that man was increasing in knowledge, and knowledge solves problems? What was he thinking? Yet he nailed it.

So what is the answer to this conundrum?

Two words must be examined in order to find the answer. *Knowledge* is the accumulation of information, while *wisdom* is the proper application of knowledge.* Mankind is addicted to knowledge and allergic to wisdom.

Let's take a look at the facts, which you can check out from a non-religious source like the Centers for Disease Control. The following is a list of societal maladies that are on the increase. Some are increasing at such a rate that it may be too late for society to pay the bill.

---

[7] Ray Stedman, *Spiritual Warfare: Winning the Daily Battle with Satan* (Word Books, 1978), 21. (Emphasis added)

Suicide

Depression

Anxiety

Insomnia

Mental health problems

Alcoholism

Drug addiction

Obesity

Bankruptcies

Hate

Riots

Wars

Divisiveness

Divorce

Lawsuits

Decline in education

Broken relationships

Homelessness

Loneliness

So much for an increase in knowledge. When knowledge is divorced from wisdom, this is the fruit of such a divorce.

We seem to hold out hope that the next computer or medical breakthrough will solve our problems. Can we just take a moment and think of the logic behind such a thought? There are approximately eight billion people on this planet. How can we ever imagine that all eight billion will one day hug and make up? You can't get ten people to get along, much less the whole world. We can't even get along with ourselves. As an old friend says, "I guess I'm just not my type.

We are literally watching the second law of thermodynamics being played out before our very eyes. This law simply says that all things are subject to decay, a process known as increasing entropy. If energy isn't put into the system, it moves from order to disorder. The Scriptures also speak to this law, how nature is subject to it but God is not: "You, Lord, laid the foundation of the earth in the beginning, and the heavens are the work of your hands; they will perish, but you remain; they will all wear out like a garment, like a robe you will roll them up, like a garment they will be changed. But you are the same, and your years will have no end" (Heb. 1:10–12). If a nation doesn't maintain moral integrity along with ethical standards, that nation will eventually decay under the weight of its own depravity. I am fully aware of the fact that the adherents of the progressive sexual revolution would say their morality is as good as mine and has the fewest restrictions. But how is that working? We have more mental trauma than ever before, which is directly linked to the violation of God's moral code. Speaking of codes, look at a few portions of the moral code for motion pictures adopted in 1930. The world sees this as antiquated and behind the times. The idea of being progressive has surely come a long way.

> **Sex:** The sanctity of the institution of marriage and the home shall be upheld. Pictures shall not infer that low forms of sex relationships are accepted or common thing.
>
> **Adultery:** Adultery, sometimes necessary plot material, must not be explicitly treated, justified, or presented attractively.
>
> **Vulgarity:** The treatment of low, disgusting, unpleasant, though not necessarily evil, subjects should always be subject

to the dictates of good taste and a regard for the sensibilities of the audience.

Obscenity: Obscenity in word, gesture, reference, song, joke, or suggestion (even when likely to be understood only by part of the audience) is forbidden.[8]

The United States is decaying in many ways Bill, as I trust you would agree. And I would suggest that *a nation doesn't rise and fall on its economy; it rises or falls on its morality, which dictates its economy.* A simple observation regarding the movie code shows how far we have fallen and continue to fall. The question is when will we hit bottom and when we do, what will that look like?

Let's think about how government spending works. A pie chart of where our tax dollars go only shows the crust, not the filling. For example, the chart may show how many billions will be spent on education. We immediately think of teacher salaries, books and maintenance of school property. But what about vandalism, counseling for unruly students, lawsuits from parents because their child didn't get straight As and may not get a college scholarship? And that's all just one wedge of the massive pie chart. But of course, if we just get our person in the White House, they will clean out the swamp.

This is where the Scriptures nail it. *We* are the swamp. As one theologian put it, the reason the world is in such a mess is that it is under poor leadership: *us.* Have you ever noticed that at every graduation, be it high school or college, the message is always the same? The speaker is usually a politician, athlete, or famous entertainer. The message is always the same, with a slight variation

---

[8] "The Motion Picture Production Code of 1930," *History Matters: The U. S. Survey Course on the Web*, George Mason University, accessed February 26, 2025, https://historymatters.gmu.edu/d/5099.

of the wording. *You're the generation that can change the world. What your mind can conceive, you can achieve.* Then they graduate and can't change a diaper.

Bill, let's talk about another reason we will never usher in utopia.

The Problem with Problems

Bill, problems have been with man ever since Adam and Eve sinned in Genesis 3. With one bad decision, the world immediately became infested with problems. Little has changed from then until now. With one careless email or tweet, relationships can immediately become entangled with strife. Problems take one second to create and a lifetime to repair the damage.

The world can't seem to see this, as political candidates keep on promising utopia when they are elected. They promise that problems will fall by the wayside once they are in the seat of power. But we have seen this movie before, Bill, and the ending is always the same: a barren wasteland of broken promises. The following is a list of reasons that problems will always have the upper hand.

1.) Problems surface immediately, while solutions take time. It is no mystery that problems arise suddenly and out of nowhere. A sudden drop in the markets due to an increase in interest rates affects your income. A new disease makes its way into society with no warning. Your new car is being recalled because of potential brake problems. These things happen on a daily basis, and solutions often require many meetings with experts who disagree on how the problem is to be solved. Meanwhile, the problems keep causing more mischief than a toddler rummaging unsupervised through an antique store.

2.) Problems are free, while solutions are expensive. There is no charge associated with problems. You won't get a bill at the end of the month because you were stuck in a traffic jam that caused you to miss an important meeting. The bill is attached to the solution. If you suddenly have a migraine, you are not charged for the migraine. But you will be charged for the visit to the doctor, followed by the trip to the pharmacist. The problem comes free of charge. The doctor and the drugs don't.

3.) **Problems are abundant, while solutions are rare.** Problems surface daily out of thin air. We experience them in every arena of life: health, finances, marriage, children, work, relationships, etc. Solutions are not waving their hands at us, saying, "Pick me, pick me." You need to work hard to find solutions. Solutions require research and can be exhausting and time-consuming.

4.) **Problems move at the speed of cheetahs, and solutions at the speed of sloths.** Problems roam the earth with impunity, leaving in their wake a host of troubles for solutions to clean up. This is observable on a daily basis. You arrive at work and are greeted with an array of problems, and your boss wants quick solutions. The printer isn't working, the server is down, and three key employees have called in sick. When you get home, you get an earful of what went on at school that wasn't fair, and then you sift through the bills with unexplained charges, which now require making phone calls not answered by humans but by computers who couldn't care less about your issues, saying, "Please select from the following menu." Don't you just love it?

5.) **Problems are always ahead of solutions, which can never catch up.** The problems are way out front of solutions, which is obvious because problems are the first cause. You don't offer solutions where there are no problems. Thus, problems will always lead the way and be in the driver's seat. Solutions will always be in the trunk, gasping for air.

6.) **Problems always outnumber solutions.** I know this is not a helpful exercise in making your day a more joyful one, but we must face the music, and the present melody is a dirge played in a minor key. Problems outweigh solutions a hundred to one. They make appearances at the most inopportune times. They are never invited to the party but show up unannounced, drawing all the attention to themselves. They are very comfortable on center stage and usually make several curtain calls the audience never encouraged.

7.) **Problems are often created by previous solutions.** Social media was designed to help people connect, but it has had the exact opposite effect. People hide behind screens and have very little social interaction. Depression is on the rise among teenagers because of the very solution social media was designed to correct. People are bullied on social media and may feel left out because they are don't get as many likes as others on Instagram.

Many affairs have begun on the internet. People's savings have been hacked into, and children have been lured into dens of darkness. Addiction to entertainment, pornography, and video games have descended upon us like an avalanche. There is no disinfectant for our problems. We have toxicity from mercury fillings, bankruptcy from credit cards, illness from preservatives, increased workload due to computers, pollution from cars and planes, virtual friends replacing real friends, inflammation from sugar, and ten thousand other maladies not anticipated with the influx of human knowledge. Where are all the solutions?

8.) **Problems can have a single source, while solutions require many.** One errant match can rally an entire fire department. One bullet can demand the attention of the city's police force. One tweet can set nation against nation. We read about these issues all the time in the news. Problems sound the alarm, creating panic, but who is called to lead the way to remedy the situation? Those who step forward often become fodder for late-night TV hosts—maybe even you, Bill. Letters to the editor will take a shot at your foolhardy approach. Problems don't draw people together but create a competitive spirit in finding the right solution. Universal problems that impact every nation are impossible to solve because of obvious barriers such as language, customs, monetary issues, religion and many more.

9.) Problems are fertile soil for blame-shifting. Are the Democrats at fault for the falling stock prices? Are the Republicans to blame for the pathetic healthcare in America? Finger-pointing has been around as long as man has had fingers. We have to find someone to blame. The blame game only adds fuel to the problems as they multiply like rabbits.

10.) Problems are no respecter of persons, families, cities, or nations. No one is immune or out of reach. And it's not hard to see why humanity is buried underneath the weight of its problems and can never catch a break. Yes, we need to do all we can to rid ourselves of disease and poverty. But the real culprit is the human heart, which man can never remedy.

The apostle Paul speaks to this issue in Romans 8, where he refers to the creation being subjected to frustration. "And not only the creation, but we ourselves, who have the first fruits of the Spirit, groan inwardly as we wait eagerly for adoption as sons, the redemption of our bodies" (Rom. 8:23).

Mankind is chasing his own tail. The world can never solve its problems, and trying to do so is like a snake attempting to throw a fastball. This is why we don't need a problem-solver but a *Savior*. Jesus did not just come to solve our problems but to give us wisdom in the midst of our problems. In the gospel of Luke, we read that "someone in the crowd said to him, 'Teacher, tell my brother to divide the inheritance with me.' But he said to him, 'Man, who made me a judge or arbitrator over you?' And he said to them, 'Take care, and be on your guard against all covetousness, for one's life does not consist in the abundance of his possessions'" (Luke 12:13–15)

In that parable, Jesus again shows us that we are the problem, and He is the solution. He is the one who redeems us from the mess we have made. Bill, that is the good news of the gospel.

The Parable of Atheism and Fertilizer

Atheism and agnosticism are very interesting takes on life. Endless debates between atheists and theists have found their way into the mainstream of society—you have participated in plenty of them yourself, Bill—with each side claiming victory and declaring the other side void of any real proof for their position. The theist sees the atheist as morally bankrupt, and the atheist sees the theist as intellectually bankrupt, with little overlap between their views.

I always do my best to simplify issues that are over my head. I would get annihilated in a debate by an atheistic philosopher or scientist. Many have exceedingly high IQs. Mine, not so much. If I were in a debate, I would do everything in my power to avoid being sucked into their intellectual narrative. I want to control the narrative. In order to do that, there would need to be some very clear definitions put on the table at the outset. The atheist knows upfront that the Christian believes in the Bible as the foundation of his faith. The believer knows that one of the tenets of atheism is that people are just chemicals. There is no spirit or soul, just chemicals.

For the sake of further discussion, let's refer to people as bags of fertilizer. I assume no atheist would have a problem with this since they define humanity through the world of chemistry.

The first question I would ask is this: Since your bag of fertilizer tells you there is no God, and my bag of fertilizer tells me there is a God, why do you care, since neither of us can control what our chemistry dictates? Why the endless arguing? Our chemicals program our fate.

The second question I would ask, and I have asked this to atheists before, is, do you have a wife, children, or close friends? No doubt they would answer in the affirmative to one of the above relationships. Have you ever said "I love you" to any of those people? "Of course," would be the reply. I would then ask, suppose the recipient of your love responded, "That's just the chemicals talking"? What would you say? When I threw that out to an atheist a few years ago, he said, "They would never say that to me." To which I responded, "Of course they wouldn't say that, because they don't believe it and neither do you."

I'm not one of those people who always comes out to be the hero of my own clever dialogues with intellectuals. I have had a few knockout punches from the other side as well. I just happen to think that if we can go back again and again to the fertilizer argument, we can avoid the mental gymnastics that cause us to fall off the intellectual balance beam again and again.

Bill, as a political satirist, you get fuming mad at politicians who lie. Why do you care? Their chemicals made them lie, just as your sodium chloride made you get angry at their lying. Athletes have apologized to the world for their infidelity. Who says adultery is wrong? Why do they feel the need to apologize when their chemistry was to blame? Are they pushing personal moral values on the rest of society? How puritanically prudish.

Hollywood goes ballistic when pirated copies of their movies are distributed. How dare they tell the world that stealing is wrong. Who made them the ethical policemen of society?

In the world of chemistry, there are no moral values, and to impose their chemical morality on the rest of us is not only self-righteous but offensive and chemically explosive. This is the slippery slope that could eventually lead a whole society to believe that lying, adultery, and stealing are wrong! Will cheating and murder be added

41

to the list? How dare they push their moral and ethical agenda on my bag of fertilizer? If we allow such people into positions of leadership, it won't be long before all our fertilizer rights will be taken away, and we will be good for nothing except keeping lawns green.

I suspect, Bill, you can sense a bit of satire mixed with sarcasm. It remains to be seen where society would wind up if there were no law. Yet if there is a law, there must be a lawgiver. The very truth revealed by the apostle Paul that states the law is written in our hearts (Rom. 2:15) is displayed by atheists who get angry when the law is violated.

When a society decides to define right and wrong on its own terms, God gives people over to their own way (Rom. 1:24). The natural consequences dictated by what we call the "law of the harvest" are soon to follow. The law of the harvest is based on Galatians 6:7, which says, "Do not be deceived: God is not mocked, for whatever one sows, that will he also reap." This law has three components:

1) **You reap *what* you sow.** Plant tomato seeds and you will reap tomatoes.

2) **You reap *more than* you sow.** You plant one seed, but hundreds of seeds will be found in the plant that grows.

3) **You reap *after* you sow.** This is the kicker. When you plant an apple seed, it takes months and years before a plant sprouts, grows, and bears fruit. People sow to the passion of their sexual desires and materialistic pleasures and years later find they have an STI, indebtedness, mental issues, or other ailments. The crop eventually comes in.

Bill, here is where people get taken by surprise. Parents, including atheists, may warn their children about an issue that has moral consequences, such as getting AIDS through sexual contact. The atheist may not care if their children are sexually active as teenagers, but they do care if their son or daughter contracts an STI. As a Christian, I would see this as a violation of God's moral law. So we want the same outcome but for different reasons.

The third part of the law is where we can get tripped up. You warn your children about the consequences of their sins, or what you might call a *mistake*. The children obey and then watch for the consequences to soon arrive in the lives of their friends who are taking their chances with alcohol, drugs, and sex. But what if the consequences fail to show right away? Those children, be they from an atheist or Christian home, could feel they were lied to. "I'm missing out" is the cry. However, as the years pass, the third part of the law of the harvest kicks in—you reap *after* you sow, sometimes much later. What is my point? That God again reveals the truth in His Word.

Yes, Bill, there are troubling things in the Bible. Believe me, I have been reading it for over fifty years; I have many questions and always will. The Scriptures admit that "there are some things in them that are hard to understand" (2 Pet. 3:16). What would we expect from an infinite God? If I had all the knowledge and wisdom of God, I would be God. The psalmists shook their fists at God. "How long, O LORD? Will you forget me forever? How long will you hide your face from me?" (Ps. 13:1). David was angry with God, as were some of the prophets. I love the Scriptures for their honesty. The Bible does not shy away from the hard issues of life, nor does it sugarcoat the struggles.

Chapter 4:

Suppressing the Truth

Mathematicians have a claim to the truth that they pride themselves in. Their science is exact with inerrant formulas. They can prove what they believe. In other words, you can prove 2+2=4. No wiggle room. Pure truth.

When a contractor cuts corners on building a house, the house is now jeopardized and within time the foundation will begin to crack. Truth is what sustains science, marriage, relationships, and life itself. You cannot outsmart the truth. Much like math, truth supports all of life and the interactions of life. Violate it and there will be repercussions. They are inescapable.

Any mistake in truth and down comes the building, the bridge, the marriage, the relationship, or the society. This is why we see things crumbling all around us. In many ways this present world is based on lies.

Jesus had a lot to say about the truth. "So, Jesus said to the Jews who had believed him, 'If you abide in my word, you are truly my disciples, and you will know the truth, and the truth will set you free'" (John 8:31–32). The implication is that if you don't know the truth, you will be in bondage. The entire universe is held together by truth. There are laws of motion, acceleration, velocity, and gravity. If the natural world is held together by truth, how much more should relationships be held together by the same? But as we can see from observation, and from Scripture, this does not work because, as Romans 3:4 says, "let God be true but every man a liar." Does this mean that no man can ever be trusted? No, but it is a reference to the fact that God never lies and man has a proclivity to do so.

Unfortunately, this has led to belief that truth is merely relative. No sane human being believes that. People don't pull up to an intersection and say to themselves, "I know the light is red, but since truth is relative, I will hit the gas." Yes, and such nonsense will escort you to the morgue. Truth is not subjective but objective, and we live by it every day. When truth is absent chaos is present.

These penetrating words from the apostle Paul have more to say about the human heart than almost any other place in Scripture: "For I am not ashamed of the gospel, for it is the power of God for salvation to everyone who believes, to the Jew first and also to the Greek. For in it the righteousness of God is revealed from faith for faith, as it is written, 'The righteous shall live by faith'" (Rom. 1:16–18).

Romans 1 takes the world on a journey and shows the downward spiral that comes when we reject God. You see, Bill, there is a trajectory every society travels on when sin enters that society. It is usually irreversible. We go from shock to toleration, toleration to acceptance, acceptance to embracing, embracing to promoting. When Clark Gable uttered the words "Frankly, my dear, I don't give a damn," in the 1939 film *Gone with the Wind*, it upset many people, and not just self-righteous religious types. Now, go back and review the trajectory of sin mentioned above and see where we have come in our language.

When I was in the eighth grade, the principal of my school was under massive pressure because of decadent behavior from the students, such as running in the hallways, sticking gum under the desks, smoking out back, pulling girls' hair, and spraying graffiti on the walls of the bathrooms. Now schools require armed guards and metal detectors to keep students safe. When God's truth is suppressed, morality in society does not improve.

Just remember the apostle Paul's words when he predicted what the last days would look like: "But understand this, that in the last days there will come times of difficulty. For people will be lovers of self, lovers of money, proud, arrogant, abusive, disobedient to their parents, ungrateful, unholy, heartless, unappeasable, slanderous, without self-control, brutal, not loving good, treacherous, reckless, swollen with conceit, lovers of pleasure rather than lovers of God, having the appearance of godliness, but denying its power. Avoid such people." (2 Tim. 3:1–5). I'd say he nailed it.

Our morality dictates our theology. Bill, one of the reasons many atheists deny the existence of God is not for lack of evidence but a desire to live freely with no one to answer to.

It is the very nature of all men to rearrange facts and terminology so as to blur the lines of morality, which helps remove the guilt from their consciences and the moral law written in their hearts. You see, Bill, suppressing what we know to be true is a way to excuse sin. *I better sleep with my girlfriend before we get married to see if we are sexually compatible. After all, you don't buy a pair of shoes without trying them on first.* All of this is what the apostle Paul refers to as suppressing or holding down the truth. According to Scripture, God holds us accountable for how we live our lives. There are at least four ways He does this:

1) **Our conscience holds us captive.** *Con* means with, and *science* means knowledge. So *conscience* means "to know with." However, we can neglect our conscience to the point that it no longer functions. The Scriptures refer to this as a seared or shipwrecked conscience (see 1 Tim 1:19).

2) **The law is written in our hearts (Rom. 2:15).** All people know that adultery and murder are wrong.

3) **Eternity is written in the hearts of all men.** Everyone has a built-in sense that there is life beyond the grave (Eccl. 3:11).

4) **God's Spirit convicts the world of sin, righteousness, and judgment (John 16:8).**

These four points conspire to bring a person to recognize his need for redemption, yet all four can be ignored because the pleasure of sin carries a powerful impulse to suppress truth.

Pull a loose thread on a beautiful garment and it won't be long before the garment is unrecognizable. A pile of thread will be staring you in the face. In ethics or morality, we pull loose threads away from the garment of God's good design. "Did God actually say . . . ?" was the first pull (Gen. 3:1), and then the unraveling began. God then "gave them up to a debased mind to do what ought not to be done" (Rom. 1:28), and people keep pulling the thread on the once beautiful garment.

Truth is now whatever is "relevant," life is disposable, God doesn't exist, gender is fluid, technology is king, authority is suspect, sex is a toy, ethics are what you want them to be, and AI decides the future, to mention just a few ways we have declared independence from God. Each of these threads makes up society as we now know it.

The question remains as to how much longer this can go on before the last thread is pulled.

Evil becomes good, and good becomes evil (see Isa. 5:20). We can see it unfold before our very eyes. We redefine words to let the sinner go free without any feelings of shame or guilt. The "narrow way" has been broadened. But before we dive into that, I want to be certain we pay careful attention to the apostle Paul's warning and revelation as to why men resist the truth.

"For the wrath of God is revealed from heaven against all ungodliness and unrighteousness of men, who by their unrighteousness suppress the truth. For what can be known about God is plain to them, because God has shown it to them" (Rom. 1:18–19).

Note carefully that it does not say men suppress or push away data, statistics, reason, or logic, but *the truth*. There is a world of difference.

Paul gives a reason that people reject what they know to be true. It is because of their unrighteousness. If truth interferes with my morality, then I will find a way to expel what I know to be true by clouding the very meaning of words. I will set up decoys to distract public attention away from the truth by using clever substitutes in order to blur the lines and blind the masses to what is really being said. It is a sleight of hand to use words in such a way that the public doesn't know which hand the truth is in.

You can tell the state of a society's morality by the words it uses to describe immorality. As culture is corrupted, drunkenness becomes "happy hour," adultery turns into an "affair" or "marital indiscretion," abortion gets referred to as "reproductive rights," and pornography is "adult entertainment." Why does this happen? Because whether people like it or not, their consciences are in a relentless pursuit to reveal right from wrong. So if the terms of evil are redefined, then it softens the blow to the conscience and dilutes the conscience's power to convict. If that goes on too long, the conscience will become seared and calloused. Our moral compass will start telling us that right is wrong, and wrong is right. Words matter, so let's make sure we are using the right ones.

The greatest marketing strategy in the history of the world produced by the advocates of the sexual revolution is: *If you don't agree with us, you are an intolerant, narrow-minded, hateful bigot living on the wrong side of history.* And it has worked beyond measure. Americans are fearful of being called narrow-minded bigots, and they will end up suppressing truth and denying reality. For example, all people who are made in the image and likeness of God—that would be all of us—know abortion is wrong. So how can anyone be "pro-choice"? Because they have suppressed what they know to be true—that human life dwells in the womb—and convinced themselves that abortion is good.

Jesus often used parables to drive home a point. A parable is a short story that comes alongside a truth **to advance its clarity**. In Luke 16, we read the parable of the unjust steward. As Jesus describes, the steward's manager was about to be fired for wasting resources. So the manager called the customers who owed his boss money and gave them a deal—give me 50 or 80 percent of what you owe, and we'll call it even. Then, the steward thought, when he's out of a job, those customers would think highly of him.

The steward was dishonest in his dealings with his employer, but his dishonesty was very clever and was thus commended by his manager. What troubles people when they read this parable is that Jesus seems to be endorsing dishonesty. But a careful reading shows He was not commending the man on his dishonesty, but on how shrewd he was *in* his dishonesty. "The master commended the dishonest manager for his shrewdness" (Luke 16:8a). And then there comes a rebuke. "For the sons of this world are more shrewd in dealing with their own generation than the sons of light" (16:8b). This parable reveals how the world leverages more energy in getting there philosophy across than do believers in getting the gospel out.

A number of years ago, I was contacted by a timeshare outfit. If I would listen to their one-hour spiel, they would fly my wife and me to Hawaii. I knew it was too good to be true and, sure enough, it was. Though I didn't fall for it, I had it confirmed from others who accepted the offer. They listened to the pitch and signed up for a trip to Hawaii. But lo and behold, the tickets could only be picked up, wait for it, in Thailand. That's right, they had to fly across the world to pick up their "free" tickets.

So I want to commend the sexual revolution's shrewd, though dishonest approach to suppressing the truth—a truth written in the hearts of all people that life in the womb is life created in the image and likeness of Almighty God. I, too, want to say that I have no hate in my heart for those with whom I disagree. Hate should not be part of the Christian vocabulary. However, I do grieve the loss of life God has created in the womb. There are other examples that host the moral decay, including Entertainment that goes well beyond the bounds of decency. Children are unrestrained in what they watch. Their brains as well as their minds have been compromised, which is well documented in *The Anxious Generation* by Jonathan Haidt, who, by the way, is an atheist.[9]

A final word to Christians, the children of "light." Be very careful not to fall for subtle but clever tactics to lure you into arguments that hold no truth. "You will know the truth, and the truth will set you free" (John 8:32).

---

[9] Jonathan Haidt, *The Anxious Generation: How the Great Rewiring of Childhood Is Causing an Epidemic of Mental Illness* (Penguin, 2024).

Chapter 5:

Life Is a Mirage

A mirage is often confused with a hallucination. Here is the difference. A hallucination is often caused by some chemical imbalance in the brain and what the person sees doesn't exist. A mirage on the other hand is something we see but is not actually there. If you stand on a hot runway and look as far as it goes you will see heat waves that look like puddles of blue water. You can photograph what doesn't even exist. It is created by light refraction. Many stories have been told about people lost in the desert or wilderness where they see water or an oasis that is not really there. I use this to describe our fallen world. I am not suggesting that what we experience isn't real. The experience is just as real as the thirsty wanderer looking for water and actually seeing it just a few hundred yards ahead. But when he arrives, it disappears. It was simply a mirage.

The book of Ecclesiastes captures this so well. The writer, most likely King Solomon, takes us on a rollercoaster ride. He keeps the reader off guard throughout the book. His never-ending refrain of "vanity of vanities, all is vanity" is the main theme of the book (e.g., Eccl. 1:2). "Vanity" here is simply another expression for smoke or vapor or breath or meaninglessness—a mirage.

Life without Jesus is a mirage. Lost humanity keeps seeing the future of technology solving our problems, or new medicines or philosophies of life that will usher in utopia. But once those advances arrive, they come with unanticipated problems. Cars and planes produce toxic exhaust; new medications have severe side effects; and the faster the computers get, the longer we are at the office, which is the very problem computers were designed to solve. We can't seem to extricate ourselves from this fallen world. Those outside of Christ are chasing the blue pond of water which is always just over the horizon.

You see Bill, the fall of man into sin is the very reason we can't escape. We are trapped in a closed system, and there is no way out. Just as we start to see the oasis we have been dreaming of, the bottom falls out. The Teacher in the book of Ecclesiastes calls out the endless refrain, "Utterly meaningless! Everything is meaningless." The book also includes the atheist's motto: "He who loves money will not be satisfied with money, nor he who loves wealth with his income; this also is vanity" (Eccl. 5:10). In other words, the heat waves of wealth create a distant view of all the wonders money can do for you, but once you have it, the mirage spoils the day.

Here is another example from Solomon: "I denied myself nothing my eyes desired; I refused my heart no pleasure. My heart took delight in all my labor, and this was the reward for all my toil. Yet when I surveyed all that my hands had done and what I had toiled to achieve, everything was meaningless, a chasing after the wind; nothing was gained under the sun." (Eccl. 2:10–11 NIV).

Solomon portrays life under the sun as a mirage. Life "under the sun" is an expression of life without God. It is a man roaming about this globe trying to find or create utopia, whether through a sexual pursuit, a materialistic pursuit, or an emotional high. It looks appealing and delightful in the distance, but once you get close, it evaporates. Our fallen nature creates these heat waves, which in turn present a beautiful picture of utopia, but once we arrive, we find it is all meaningless.

After his third Super Bowl win, former NFL quarterback Tom Brady told *60 Minutes*, "God, it's gotta be more than this. I mean this can't be what it's all cracked up to be. I mean I've done it. I'm 27. And what else is there for me? . . . I wish I knew."[10]

Now he has seven rings, but it still wasn't enough. It was a mirage, and it forced him to decide between pursuing his family and pursuing another Super Bowl ring. The ring was a mirage but his divorce was a sad reality.

Who are the most attractive, rich, and talented people in the world? Movie stars, hands down. They have it all, including a lot of broken marriages. Apparently, wealth, good looks, and talent fade rapidly once all three are experienced.

So where does this first show up?

> Now the serpent was more crafty than any other beast of the field that the Lord God had made. He said to the woman, "Did God actually say, 'You shall not eat of any tree in the garden'?" And the woman said to the serpent, "We may eat of the fruit of the trees in the garden, but God said, 'You shall not eat of the fruit of the tree that is in the midst of the garden, neither shall you touch it, lest you die.'" But the serpent said to the woman, "You will not surely die. For God knows that when you eat of it your eyes will be opened, and you will be like God, knowing good and evil." (Gen. 3:4–5)

Did you catch the mirage? *You will be like God.* In one sense, they would, but certainly not in the way Satan led them to believe. The mirage through a piece of fruit produced death. The mirage is nothing more than bait with a hook inside. A lure, if you will.

In our time, advertising creates a mirage. We are enticed with gadgets and gizmos and foods and fashions that we just "have to

---

[10] Daniel Schorn, "Transcript: Tom Brady, Part 3," *60 Minutes* interview, CBS News, November 4, 2005, https://www.cbsnews.com/news/transcript-tom-brady-part-3.

have." But where does all that stuff soon end up? In the dump or a garage sale.

The lottery has proven to be one of the biggest mirages of our time. A number of years back there was a story of a man by the name of Jack Whittaker, who won 315 million dollars on the Powerball jackpot. But this love for money set the stage for one tragedy after another. By the end of his life, Whittaker had lost everything. People came out of the woodwork wanting money, followed by lawsuits and the loss of friends and family.[11]

The Bible anticipates these mirages as well: "But those who desire to be rich fall into temptation, into a snare, into many senseless and harmful desires that plunge people into ruin and destruction. For the love of money is a root of all kinds of evils. It is through this craving that some have wandered away from the faith and pierced themselves with many pangs Those" (1 Tim. 6:9–10).

It is easy to go through life and push away the reality of eternity. This is one of the reasons we have to keep ourselves busy and drown out the inner conviction that eternity is deeply embedded in our hearts.

---

[11] John Raby, "From Powerball winner to scandal: Jack Whittaker dies at 72," Associated Press, June 30, 2020, https://apnews.com/article/wv-state-wire-lifestyle-ap-top-news-us-news-obituaries-97c2aae5522a9d39ef5e5bbfa2d364d0.

Chapter 6:

Biblical Psychology

Bill, there has never been a book written with such insight into the human condition as the Bible. Mankind, try as he will, cannot make life better. Sure, we can travel faster now than in days past, and we have better medicine that add years to our life expectancy. But adding years in some respects only adds to the sorrow.

Let's see if we can put the Scriptures to the test on what they say about the human heart (or chemical makeup if that suits you better). Jeremiah the prophet said, "The heart is deceitful above all things, and desperately wicked; Who can know it?" (Jer. 17:9 NKJV). And Jesus said, "Do you not see that whatever goes into the mouth passes into the stomach and is expelled? But what comes out of the mouth proceeds from the heart, and this defiles a person. For out of the heart come evil thoughts, murder, adultery, sexual immorality, theft, false witness, slander. These are what defile a person." (Matt. 15:17–20).

Let's take a look at a typical scenario. Bill, see if you can relate to this narrative. Two hundred years ago, a man goes down to catch a stagecoach and just misses it. He asks the ticket agent when the next coach will come. "Two weeks!" shouts the agent. "Two weeks?!" screams the traveler as he heads back home, cursing all the way. But thank our lucky stars for technology, his son goes down to catch a train but just misses it. He asks when the next one will be. "Two days," comes the response from the booth. "Two days?!" flies from the mouth of the traveler as he curses all the way home. But thank goodness for technology. Bill, his son goes to the airport only to find he just missed the flight. "When is the next one?" queries the disgruntled passenger. "In two hours," comes the reply. "Two hours?!" screams the would-be passenger. "I need to be at a meeting in LA today!" He storms off to the airport Starbucks, orders a latte, and fumes while he puts on his noise-canceling headset and watches a movie during a mental breakdown. But thank goodness for technology, his son rolls out of bed and heads to his computer, which reminds him the download might take two minutes. "Two minutes?! Who has that kind of time?" From two weeks to two days to two hours to two minutes, technology has changed, but here again we see what Scripture says about the human heart—it is never satisfied.

The reality is that "never satisfied are the eyes of man" (Prov. 27:20). Thus, man is filled with sinful behavior and is capable of committing any sin at any time. How many times have we heard the three words "enough is enough" from politicians or civic leaders following a serious threat that has been carried out against our society? Racism, school shootings, violence in the streets, and other man-made disasters always trigger these famous three words yet apparently enough is not enough. But when will enough actually be enough? I have always wondered why unbelievers, and often believers, continue to believe we are on the verge of erasing *enough*. There will always be wars and rumors of wars until Christ returns. When that happens, "enough is enough" will be replaced by the one who truly is enough.

Rejection of God is never intellectual but moral: By nature, Bill, we don't like to be under authority as this limits our moral and ethical freedom. No one wants to be told what they can watch and who they can sleep with. Salesmen don't like being told they can't lie about their product in order to close the deal. Our political leaders do not tend to be known for living by the teachings of Jesus found in the Sermon on the Mount. Imagine if they did—this would be a very different world.

Here again, Bill, the Scriptures reveal several truths about the nature of mankind. Everyone has a conscience to let them know right from wrong, though the conscience can be ignored to the point that it no longer knows the difference. This is what happens when we suppress the truth. Everyone has the law of God written in their hearts (Rom. 2:12–16). Everyone has eternity written in their hearts (Eccl. 3:11). Everyone has been convicted by God's Spirit revealing to them there is a judgment to come (John 16:8).

Bill, you can push back on all these, but there was a time when you knew this was true (Rom. 1:21). Everyone knows there is a God. There is a tendency to suppress these truths because of unrighteousness. We don't want to be held accountable to anyone. Religion can become bondage to a set of rules laid down by an angry imaginary god. But the truth is that people are in bondage to religion, philosophy, and political views, all of which have produced guilt, shame, depression, and fear. All unbelievers have a standard they believe in but cannot keep. That is why rules fail every time. In the world of religion, people try to keep rules in order to please their god, but they fail with every attempt. Jesus said, "You will know the truth, and the truth will set you free" (John 8:32). What does it mean to be free from a biblical sense? We are free from the fear of death. "Since therefore the children share in flesh and blood, [Jesus] himself likewise partook of the same things, that through death he might destroy the one who has the power of death, that is, the devil, and deliver all those who through fear of death were subject to lifelong slavery" (Heb. 2:14–15). We no longer fear where we will spend eternity. If you fear eternity and where you might end up, then you don't understand the freedom that comes with believing in the finished work of Christ.

"There is therefore now no condemnation for those who are in Christ Jesus. For the law of the Spirit of life has set you free in Christ Jesus from the law of sin and death" (Rom. 8:1–2). Many want to challenge this by believing that man can now live any way he wants. You don't get well to go to the hospital; you go to the hospital to get well. You don't get better to get saved; you get saved to get better. Religion has it backwards.

Chapter 7:

A Biblical View of Salvation

Bill, allow me to give you a picture of what the Bible means by "salvation." It might surprise you. I can assure you that many professing Christians do not know what I am getting ready to reveal. I hope they will enter your living room and listen to my spiritual diatribe much the way you come unglued regarding religion and politics. I fully realize you can mock the existence of God and His Word by selecting portions of Scripture out of context. But according to Scripture itself, the Bible was written for one singular purpose: "to make you wise for salvation through faith in Christ Jesus" (2 Tim 3:15). You see, Bill, the natural tendency for all men is to think they are really good people. But the Bible tells us that we all need salvation.

The skeptic says religion is a crutch. They nailed it. Religion *is* a crutch. You have one good leg and one bad leg, so you lean into religion as the crutch to support the bad leg. However, biblical Christianity tells a different story. The biblical gospel says, "As it is written: 'There is none righteous, no, not one; there is none who understands; there is none who seeks after God. They have all turned aside; They have together become unprofitable; there is none who does good, no, not one'" (Rom. 3:10–12).

According to this passage, both legs are bad—which means we don't need a crutch but a stretcher! That stretcher is a Person: Jesus. He is the one who carries us through life and into the eternal Kingdom. Ask the average person if they are certain they will go to heaven when they die? The typical response is, "I hope so." (Not a good answer). Or, "I have never hurt anyone, and I'm a good person" (Not a good answer.) Or, "I go to church and give money when the plate comes by." Nice try, but God is not impressed. God is impressed with His Son. "And a voice from heaven said, "this is my Son, whom I love; with him I am well pleased" (Matt. 3:17). He is impressed with the person who says I am not good and have nothing to offer you in the way of good works. God doesn't want us to *hope* so, but to *know* so.

You see, Bill, religious people have an imaginary collection of spiritual merit badges they sow onto their spiritual vest. However, the biblical gospel presents another view. The book of Romans drags the world into a courtroom and declares all are guilty. God is perfect and has perfect laws we are to keep. The problem is that no one can keep them. *The law commands perfect righteousness and condemns our every attempt to achieve it.* The pope can't perfectly keep God's law. Billy Graham couldn't. Not even Mother Teresa. "None is righteous, no, not one; no one understands; no one seeks for God. All have turned aside; together they have become worthless; no one does good, not even one" (Rom 3:10).

That is a very strong indictment. Those are hard words, but they are true. Paul is not saying that everyone is as bad as they can be, but they are as bad off as they can be.

Any attempt to rely on one's human goodness and display your spiritual letter sweater on the day of judgment will be met with these words from Jesus: "I never knew you; depart from me, you workers of lawlessness" (Matt. 7:22–23). Trying to earn salvation means good works do not lead to good news.

The reason for such a harsh response is that to rely on your goodness is to say to Jesus, "You didn't do enough. Your sacrifice was not sufficient; therefore, I will supplement Your sacrifice with my good works." We think that this will close the gap, and our chances of entering His kingdom will be fairly secure. Every true believer in Christ can have the complete assurance of entering the kingdom of God at the moment they believe the gospel. That is why the gospel is good news. It is not good news to be left in the dark about where you will spend eternity. "I am the resurrection and the life. Whoever believes in me, though he die, yet shall he live, and everyone who lives and believes in me shall never die. Do you believe this?" (John 11:25–26). The Lord never intended us to doubt where we will go when we die. Listen to these words from the apostle John: "I write these things to you who believe in the name of the Son of God, that you may *know* that you have eternal life" (1 John 5:13, emphasis added). For me to say I know that when I die I will go directly into His final kingdom can be perceived as arrogance. They think I'm bragging about how good I am. Scripture debunks that idea when it says, "For by grace you have been saved through faith. And this is not your own doing; it is the gift of God, not a result of works, so that no one may boast" (Eph. 2:8–9).

Here is another one that pulls the rug out from under our self-righteousness. "He saved us, not because of works done by us in righteousness, but according to his own mercy, by the washing of regeneration and renewal of the Holy Spirit" (Titus 3:5). If that is not enough, try this one on for size: "To the one who does not work but believes in him who justifies the ungodly, his faith is counted as righteousness" (Rom. 4:5).

You can see why Karl Marx referred to religion as the opiate of the masses. He was right. Religion is a drug to make people feel good about themselves. But the aforementioned verses are designed to remove our exalted view of ourselves and humble us to where we rest fully in Christ for our salvation. Bill, this may all be new to you, as it is with many professing believers. God has never and will never let *good* people into His kingdom. He only lets perfect people in. Jesus and the apostle Paul state emphatically that there are no good people. Jesus said to a rich young man who called Him good, "Why do you call me good? No one is good except God alone" (Mark 10:18). So, Jesus is either God or He is not good. God is not opposed to good works, especially when they flow from our appreciation for Him saving us, but He is strongly opposed to our reliance on good works for saving ourselves.

But what the above Scriptures are saying is how unqualified we are to enter God's presence since heaven is a place of perfection, and my sin will pollute it; thus, I can't enter. So how am I able to come in? I'm glad you asked. Those who go to heaven enter in on the perfect righteousness of another—namely Christ. Listen to these words by the apostle Paul: "For our sake he made him to be sin who knew no sin, so that in him we might become the righteousness of God" (2 Cor. 5:21). This is the great exchange. He takes on my sin, and I take on His righteousness. Many people who call themselves Christians will tell you that no one can be certain in this world that they have eternal life. Yet the Scriptures beg to differ. Listen to the recorded testimony of those in scripture.

King David said, "Surely goodness and mercy shall follow me all the days of my life, and I shall dwell in the house of the Lord forever" (Ps. 23:6).

Asaph said, "You guide me with your counsel, and afterward you will receive me to glory" (Ps. 73:24).

Job said, "For I know that my redeemer lives, and at the last he will stand upon the earth. And after my skin has been thus destroyed, yet in my flesh I shall see God" (Job 19:25–26).

Paul said, "For to me to live is Christ, and to die is gain. If I am to live in the flesh, that means fruitful labor for me. Yet which I shall choose I cannot tell. I am hard pressed between the two. My desire is to depart and be with Christ, for that is far better" (Phil. 1:21–23)

To the thief on the cross, Jesus said, "Truly, I say to you, today you will be with me in paradise" (Luke 23:43).

Jesus said, "Nevertheless, do not rejoice in this, that the spirits are subject to you, but rejoice that your names are written in heaven" (Luke 10:20).

All of these passages show us that it is possible, in this world, to be assured of eternal life. The thief on the cross had no time to get baptized and start living a good life. All he did was believe. And what did Jesus say to him? "*Today* you will be with me in paradise." Those lacking in assurance are trusting in something other than Christ alone. Time to trust and gain assurance.

You see, Bill, religion is pride before the law ("Look at how good I am by keeping the law!"), while biblical Christianity is *humility before the cross* ("I have nothing to offer but to admit my need for the Savior."). Bill, for you and anyone else who is reading this, I want to ask you a question that goes back many years: If you died today and stood before God, and He asked why He should let you in to heaven, what would you say? If you start with "Because I . . .," you are in deep trouble. If you start with "Because You . . .," you are on the right track. Christ paid it all.

Bill, that is a very brief summary of a biblical understanding of the gospel. As I said at the beginning of this book, I respect your honesty. Let me return the favor. I tell young pastors that when they are preparing their sermons, they should ask themselves what questions people would ask if they were given a mic. And then answer those questions in the sermon. I think I can anticipate what you and others might ask me over a cup of coffee about this book. I believe I would hear something like this: "Hey, Mike, way to go giving us all the amazing facts about Scripture. Very impressive, but you avoided the hard issues in Scripture, like the killing of the Canaanites and the persistence of evil and horrible diseases that prevail all over the world." The simple reason I didn't go into those issues is that they have been dealt with by plenty of great scholars over the centuries. The Christian world does not have all the answers, nor do we claim to have them. If I tried to hit all the hard issues, we would be here forever, going down every rabbit hole. The Bible was written to let us know what God wants us to know. Do I have questions for God? You bet I do. Lots of them. Having pastored for over fifty years, I have seen some great hardships.

It was Mark Twain who supposedly said, "It ain't the parts of the Bible that I can't understand that bothers me. It is the parts that I do understand."

But let me flip that on its head: *It's what I do understand about the Bible that convinces me that what I don't understand must have a reasonable explanation.*

One-third of the psalms are laments. God doesn't hide from the hardships of life. He is very real about tragedies, but rarely, if ever, does He tell us why they are happening. He only says He is with us, and I have observed that to be true as I have seen many people walk by faith in very difficult times. Yes, I have my doubts from time to time, but the Lord gives me great hope as I study the Scriptures. So, what do I do when I don't understand? I put my questions into five buckets.

Bucket Number One: When I just don't understand, I go to Deuteronomy 29:29, which states, "The secret things belong to the Lord our God, but the things that are revealed belong to us and to our children forever, that we may do all the words of this law." I find this comforting because the Lord is letting me know I can't understand everything with my finite mind. There are companion verses such as Romans 11:33, which says, "Oh, the depth of the riches and wisdom and knowledge of God! How unsearchable are his judgments and how inscrutable his ways!"

Another of my favorites is Isaiah 55:8–9: "For my thoughts are not your thoughts, neither are your ways my ways, declares the Lord.

For as the heavens are higher than the earth, so are my ways higher than your ways and my thoughts than your thoughts."

Bucket Number Two: In 1 Corinthians 13:12, we read, "For now we see in a mirror dimly, but then face to face. Now I know in part; then I shall know fully, even as I have been fully known."

Here, we find there are things in life we can know but not fully.

Bucket Number Three: Referring to the writings of Paul, the apostle Peter says, "He writes the same way in all his letters, speaking in them of these matters. His letters contain some things that are hard to understand, which ignorant and unstable people distort, as they do the other Scriptures, to their own destruction" (NIV).

This verse tells me there are things in Scripture that I *can* understand but are troubling. So here we have the apostle Peter admitting even he struggles. If he struggled, then certainly I will.

Bucket Number Four: In John 16:12, Jesus says to His disciples, "I still have many things to say to you, but you cannot bear them now." I think He means they are not mature enough to handle certain revelations.

Bucket Number Five: That which is clear.

The Bible is a very complex book. There are many doctrinal statements that are clear and others that are not as clear. Salvation by grace through faith in Christ alone is beyond clear. The virgin birth, the resurrection, and the eventual return of Christ are revealed with great clarity.

Bill, no one has all the answers to all the revelation of scripture. We are talking about the mind of God, and no one will ever plumb the depths of His wisdom. Jesus said, "He who has ears, let him hear" (Matt. 13:9). We must have an illuminated mind to understand the word of God. We can pray with the psalmist, "Open my eyes, that I may behold wondrous things out of your law" (Ps. 119:18).

Chapter 8:

A Theology of Life

Bill, permit me to give you the biblical view of life, and we can see how it compares with the atheistic view.

The natural and supernatural views of life on earth both require a miracle. If God simply spoke and the worlds were framed, that is certainly a miracle (Heb. 11:3). Yet the humanistic understanding is that life formed in thermal vents or from lightning striking primordial soup millions of years ago. That sure sounds like a miracle because, no matter how you look at it, life coming from non-life is an impossibility. Scientists have never been able to observe or replicate the origin of life. So when such an impossibility occurs, we call that a miracle.

The Bible never presents the world as a perfectly happy, fun place to live. As we have discussed, Bill, the search for utopia on earth is always in vain. The reason for this is that man, since the sin of Adam is not basically good. Jesus said that as time goes on, "You will hear of wars and rumors of wars. . . . For nation will rise against nation, and kingdom against kingdom, and there will be famines and earthquakes in various places" (Matt. 24:6–7).

And about the wickedness inherent in all of us, He said, "What comes out of a person is what defiles him. For from within, out of the heart of man, come evil thoughts, sexual immorality, theft, murder, adultery, coveting, wickedness, deceit, sensuality, envy, slander, pride, foolishness. All these evil things come from within, and they defile a person" (Mark 7:20–23).

We don't like to hear this of ourselves, but we know it's true, don't we, Bill? Not everyone commits all of these sins, but the potential is within everyone, and what has not been carried out has been imagined in our hearts.

In 2024, *USA Today* reported that a Michigan man killed his neighbor over an argument about mulch.[12] Now pause for a moment and let that sink in. Both men got up that morning with no intent to start an argument. One was murdered and the other imprisoned. You can be sure the neighbors were in shock. It's possible that both men were seen as good guys, but the heat of the moment sparked a violent altercation. Probably none of the neighbors would have thought they had a murderer on their street.

Unfortunately, such an incident is not that rare. We see things like that in the news on a daily basis. The news simply reports how bad humanity was the day before. Here is another verse from Scripture that we don't like to hear: "The heart is deceitful above all things, and desperately wicked; who can know it?" (Jer. 17:9 NKJV)? It all started with Cain murdering Abel over a sacrifice offered to God. Now we have people be killed in quiet neighborhoods over mulch. We are surprised by what the human heart is capable of, though we read about it every day.

We also experience it in our own lives. How many times do we go to bed thinking about some awful thing we did and ask ourselves, "What was I thinking?" I guess my question for the humanist would be, if evolution is true and evolution moves in a positive direction, how could this innocent primordial microscopic cell carry within its DNA such evil? Here is the biblical answer: "Therefore, just as sin

---

[12] Julia Gomez, "Michigan father killed in shooting over reported argument about mulch; neighbor charged," *USA Today*, August 14, 2024, https://www.usatoday.com/story/news/nation/2024/08/14/michigan-father-shot-killed-neighbor-charged/74793204007.

came into the world through one man, and death through sin, and so death spread to all men because all sinned" (Rom. 5:12).

Bill, I know this sounds strange to the natural mind, but just look around. The Scriptures nail it at every turn.

Why do we lie? Because we believe the outcome will be better than if we tell the truth. So when schools of higher learning and governments lie to their people, we will have a world that cannot maintain any form of cohesiveness. In reality, everything is held together by the iron backbone of truth as opposed to a spider web of lies. Where there is no truth there is disintegration. Buildings and bridges collapse if the engineers cut corners on truthful calculations. So it is not hard to see why the world continues to spoil under the weight of its own lack of integrity and a conscience that no longer functions.

So what do humans do to assuage their conscience? They invent religions. And as was said earlier, religion is a drug to keep the gods from being mad at us. And here is why. The biblical gospel sympathizes with us. The word gospel means good news. It is not good news Bill if we don't have the assurance of eternal life. A lack of certainty means the professing believer is trusting something or someone other than Jesus being their sole sufficiency.

God has employed four pressure points to get the attention of all people, even those who do not believe in Him.

1. Ecclesiastes 3:11 says that eternity is written in the hearts of all men. Since we have eternal souls there is a sense of eternity.
2. God has sent His Spirit to "convict the world concerning sin and righteousness and judgment" (John 16:8).
3. We crave justice. Why? Not because of chemistry but because the law is written in our hearts (Rom. 2:15). We know right from wrong.

4. Whether people like it or not, their consciences are in a relentless pursuit to reveal right from wrong, though the conscience can become seared if it is ignored (Titus 1:15).

So God uses the heart, the conscience, and His Holy Spirit to arouse the attention of the human soul. God has given us natural revelation through the universe that screams of His creative powers, coupled with specific revelation of His Word. Scientists, philosophers, and educators labor diligently trying to figure out how to quell the evil in the human heart, but to no avail. This is why God has provided a gospel in which man can be saved, taken out of the kingdom of darkness and placed into the kingdom of God's dear Son, where man can pass from death unto life, where man can be born again.

Those expressions are statements of release and genuine freedom. The gospel and the life of Christ are too complicated to be invented by man. The Scriptures and their wisdom are well beyond the world of human wisdom. "Where is the one who is wise? Where is the scribe? Where is the debater of this age? Has not God made foolish the wisdom of the world? 21 For since, in the wisdom of God, the world did not know God through wisdom, it pleased God through the folly of what we preach to save those who believe" (1 Cor. 1:20–21).

Compare the wisdom of the world with the Sermon on The Mount (Matt. 5–7), or these words from Jesus, when He said, "And this is the judgment: the light has come into the world, and people loved the darkness rather than the light because their works were evil" (John 3:19).

No truer words have ever been spoken, Bill. The Bible looks far beyond the world of philosophy, psychiatry, and psychology. It takes us to the depths of our depravity, and it makes us uncomfortable. Jesus says the reason the world hates Him is because He testifies of its evil (John 7:7). But Jesus doesn't hate the world—He knows our condition and wants to rescue us from ourselves. Bill, you might be asking, "How does He rescue us?" I thought you'd never ask . . .

Chapter 9:

The Conclusion of the Matter

Bill, the resurrection of Jesus Christ is the climax of all human history. Let's see if we can trace the importance of this miraculous event. At face value, this would seem to be another one of those "silly" Bible stories, that a dead man would rise from the grave.

But keep in mind that in a fable, none of the facts hold together because it is made up, and truth is irrelevant. When truth is not the centerpiece of all dialogue, the dialogue is not worth having. The resurrection is much different. There have been volumes written by former atheists (like Lee Strobel) on the compelling evidence for this miracle of all miracles. I have no desire to cover what has already been covered far better by others. My objective is to show why this event is necessary. No one would write such nonsense if there were no compelling context to the biblical narrative.

Remember, Bill, God told Adam and Eve that when they ate of the forbidden fruit they would surely die. They ate, they immediately died spiritually, and they began to die physically. The Lord could not just overlook the offense and move on—justice must be satisfied—so He set up a rescue plan. Adam and Eve violated the law of God, and since the wages of sin is death (Rom. 6:23), someone had to die. No mere human could step in because all of Adam's descendants would be tainted with sin. We needed a sinless Savior. And that is why Jesus had to have both a human and a divine nature—we needed a man to pay our penalty of rebellion against God, but we needed God to be able to perfectly keep the law that we could not keep. Such a story could never have been written by any human.

When Christ came out of the grave, He showed His power over death, which the Bible refers to as "the last enemy to be destroyed" (1 Cor. 15:26). The resurrection of Christ is hinted at in the Old Testament, as we saw in the narratives of Isaac and Jonah. And it was gloriously fulfilled in the New Testament. You see, Bill, the Bible has layer upon layer of themes you can trace that are all related to the story of redemption. That is what I have been trying to show throughout this book.

But to see how it all fits together, one must read the Bible and be acquainted with its themes. For the first twenty-six years of my life, I had never looked inside the Bible and was of the impression that it was just a moral handbook—if I kept my nose clean, my human goodness and church attendance would get me into heaven. Eventually, I found out that such a mindset is completely antithetical to the Scriptures. I have no human goodness. Listen to these words about Jesus: "But when the goodness and loving kindness of God our Savior appeared, he saved us, not because of works done by us in righteousness, but according to his own mercy, by the washing of regeneration and renewal of the Holy Spirit, whom he poured out on us richly through Jesus Christ our Savior" (Titus 3:4–6).

Salvation has zero to do with us. We cannot save ourselves. It is completely a work of God. In the book of Isaiah, we read these words: "But we are all like an unclean thing, and all our righteousness are like filthy rags; we all fade as a leaf, and our iniquities, like the wind, have taken us away" (Isa. 64:6 NKJV).

And the apostle Paul writes, "But whatever gain I had, I counted as loss for the sake of Christ. Indeed, I count everything as loss because of the surpassing worth of knowing Christ Jesus my Lord. For his sake I have suffered the loss of all things and count them as rubbish, in order that I may gain Christ" (Phil. 3:7–8).

So, Scripture comes hard after the religious person who thinks their church attendance, financial giving, and good deeds will give them a better chance of entering the kingdom. God has a very different view. The Bible says that our human goodness is "filthy rags" or "rubbish."

This is really brutal language. But the Lord uses such language to get the attention of the self-righteous person. When I first heard the gospel in the summer of 1970, I was traumatized. All those years of trying my best to earn God's favor, only to find I was working my way further from God.

In Romans, the apostle Paul writes, "Now to the one who works, his wages are not counted as a gift but as his due. And to the one who does not work but believes in him who justifies the ungodly, his faith is counted as righteousness" (Rom. 4–5).

Are you perfectly righteous in the eyes of God Bill? If not, there is a way (and only one way) you can be. Here is one of the clearest statements anywhere in Scripture: "God made him who had no sin to be sin for us, so that in him we might become the righteousness of God" (2 Cor. 5:21).

Did you catch that? When we put our faith in Christ and not our righteousness, we actually become as righteous as God Himself. God has never let anyone into heaven without being clothed in the righteousness of Christ Himself. God has never, and will never, let "good people" into heaven. He only lets in *perfect* people in. And since none of us is perfect, we need the perfection of Christ placed to our account. In June of 1970, I was declared perfect in the eyes of God. Thus, when I die, I have the assurance that I will go directly into His final kingdom as a sinless person. That is why the word *gospel* means good news.

The Bible says, "For by grace you have been saved through faith. And this is not your own doing; it is the gift of God, not a result of works, so that no one may boast" (Eph. 2:8–9). Have you received the gift, Bill? If not, why not?

Bill, I want to make sure you don't miss the point: Jesus Christ died a death we couldn't die and lived a life we couldn't live. His sacrifice thus satisfied the righteous demands of God the Father. This is not a silly story—it is life and death. And believing in Christ and His payment for your sin is the only way to enter into His eternal presence in heaven.

Wrapping It Up

Bill, my objective has not been to act like I have all the answers to life and the universe. But, in this short book, I have tried to show some of the reasons why I believe the Bible is divinely inspired, why it can be trusted, and how it shows us the way to eternal salvation. We've seen how the Bible makes all kinds of "lucky guesses" about nature and humanity—about the makeup of the universe, the nautical design of the ark, the formation of the nation of Israel, the decline of morality, and more. I hope you scratched your head a few times and said to yourself, "Now there is something I never knew." You certainly cannot just cast it all off as if there is no cogent argument. I certainly don't cast off your arguments. You make me think and make me think hard. It forces me to sharpen my pencil and drives me back to the drawing board. I don't blindly believe the Bible. I'm a skeptic by nature, but the Scriptures reveal the truth of human nature and why we fail to lift ourselves up by our own bootstraps. It tells us why we are on a treadmill picking up speed day by day going nowhere faster and faster. Bill, you may feel no need to answer to a God you don't believe in, but you will forever answer to your conscience. It will never leave you alone, though you can push it away enough times that it will give up trying. Yes, there will be push back by those who don't want to believe. However, any honest skeptic will either have to stop being honest or stop being a skeptic based on what has been presented in this book. No, I am not claiming infallibility but a certain degree of credibility that cannot be ignored.

The Bible is God's revelation to man. But here is the big question: Have you, or anyone reading this, come to the place of calling upon the Lord that they would be given everlasting life? Bill, I hope someday we can meet. I think we would enjoy ribbing each other. But my supreme desire is that one day I can call you brother and that you will find "Real Time" with God.

Mike

Appendix

Entering the World of the Unknown

The Bible was not written to tell us what we can discover through our five human senses. It was written to tell us what our illuminated sixth sense discerns. This is called "revelation." And it means entering into the world of the unknown. Bill, I want to give you a list of things that are revealed in Scripture that we would otherwise not know.

1) **We would never know why education without wisdom is a dead-end street.** Education is the pursuit of knowledge. Wisdom is the proper application of knowledge. This is proven daily in all schools of higher education. Remove the wisdom of Scripture and life dies a slow death. Just read today's news, or tomorrow's, it's all the same.

2) **We would never know that the heart is incurably wicked (Jer.17:9).** *What was I thinking? How did I get into this mess? Why did we get a divorce? I never thought I would be in jail for such stupidity. Alcohol has taken over. I'm committing adultery on the internet and can't seem to stop. My conscience won't leave me alone.* I am filled with guilt and shame. All these are true of atheists, Muslims, Catholics, Protestants, Hindus, Buddhists, and more. We all have ways of trying to push our conscience off a cliff by clever excuses and justifying our behavior

3) **We would never know there are two kingdoms at war with one another, the kingdom of darkness and the kingdom of light.** "He has delivered us from the domain of darkness and transferred us to the kingdom of his beloved Son, in whom we have redemption, the forgiveness of sins" (Col. 1:13–14). Yes, Bill, there are two kingdoms. If people are

outside of Christ, they are in the kingdom of darkness. There is a sense that their grit and guts will get them through this messed-up world. But look at the two elements the world of darkness is dependent on: evolution and intelligence. These two factors should have delivered society from its troubles, but it only gets worse by the day. That is why it is called the kingdom of darkness.

4) **We would never know we have an enemy.** As someone once said, "The world couldn't be this bad without some outside help." The Bible tells us where that help comes from. "For we do not wrestle against flesh and blood, but against the rulers, against the authorities, against the cosmic powers over this present darkness, against the spiritual forces of evil in the heavenly places" (Eph. 6:12). That's right, Bill, the world is under Satanic influence, which explains why the world is trapped in evil and its consequences. Every industry, government, religion, and business is tainted with lies and deception. No president or leader of any country will rid that country of corruption. All presidents in their inaugural address paint themselves as a messiah, even as their administration continues to marinate in corruption. Bill, this is where you so often step up to the plate and call these people out.

5) **We would never know about the world, the flesh, and the devil.** These three conspire to control all societies. The flesh is not our physical skin and bones, but is used in Scripture to describe our self-centeredness, our lust, greed, anger and hatred etc. We are all aware of our shortcomings. The Bible calls it *sin*. Jesus said, "And this is the judgment: the light has come into the world, and people loved the darkness rather than the light because their works were evil" (John 3:19). The Bible uses the word "darkness" to describe man's inability to know the God of all creation. Man is by nature blinded to the truth of the gospel and invents religion to assuage his conscience. The most pernicious lie that has ever

been cast at the feet of humankind is that man can earn salvation through good works. The entire theme of Scripture is that man is separated from a holy God and cannot save himself but his nature is that he needs a little skin in the game to help Jusus out. This is a deadly and false teaching. When the Philippian jailor asked Paul, "What must he do to be saved?" Paul responded with, "Believe in the Lord Jesus, and you will be saved" (Acts 16:30–31).

6) **We would never know why man can't seem to fix his problems.** Earlier in this book, we talked about the "problem with problems." Perhaps a tad more on the subject will be helpful. Bill, just look around at the world and all the brilliant scientists, mathematicians, medical experts, psychologist, psychiatrists, counselors, and engineers, but the needle hasn't moved regarding fixing the human heart. I'm not talking about the one that pumps blood, but the one that holds our emotions and brings tears to our eyes, the immaterial part of us that we think and feel with. Every atheist has built into his emotional reservoir the same feelings. This world is a place of hurt, but God never intended that from His original creation. Seven times in Genesis one the Lord says that what he made was good.

7) **We would never know that man is the problem.** And as we mentioned earlier, when the problem tries to solve the problem, that's a problem. You see, Bill, if we were to look at the history of civilization, we would soon find that jealousy—the fear of being replaced on the world stage— along with envy—I want what you have—create massive, unsolvable problems. All of man's solutions come up short, or create new problems. For example, seeking help through AI in the world of medicine may prove to be of great benefit, but AI cannot penetrate the human soul because AI can only work within the bounds of that which is tangible, and the soul is immaterial. I realize this is a world that you do not embrace, but I truly believe that you and many others know

it is true but fear surrendering to Almighty God. The Bible, "For although they knew God, they did not honor him as God or give thanks to him, but they became futile in their thinking, and their foolish hearts were darkened" (Rom. 1:21).

8) **We would never know the nature of sin and its consequences.** What is sin? It is the transgression of the law of God (1 John 3:4). People can reject the idea of a moral standard, but it is written on their hearts (Rom. 2:15). Bill, this is why atheists hate lying, theft, murder, and greed just the way a Christ follower does. Where else could this standard come from, except a Holy God?

9) **We would never know that the wisdom of this world is foolishness with God.** "For the wisdom of this world is folly with God. For it is written, 'He catches the wise in their craftiness'" (1 Cor. 3:19). Man is blinded to biblical wisdom, so he leans on his own understanding, which is exactly what Proverbs 3:5–6 says not to do: "Trust in the LORD with all your heart, and do not lean on your own understanding. In all your ways acknowledge him, and he will make straight your paths." And King David said, "I am a stranger in the earth; do not hide Your commandments from me" (Ps. 119:19 NKJV). The gist of what David is saying is that we don't belong here. The Scriptures refer to believers in Christ as strangers, pilgrims, aliens, and sojourners in this world. The wisdom of the world is foolishness because our true citizenship is a heavenly one. "But our citizenship is in heaven, and from it we await a Savior, the Lord Jesus Christ, who will transform our lowly body to be like his glorious body, by the power that enables him even to subject all things to himself" (Phil. 3:20–21).

10) **We would never know there is a heaven and a hell.** Though hell is debated by theologians, they would agree it is a place you don't want to go. It is where justice is meted out by an all-knowing and just God. No one escapes His just scales as

every word and deed will be brought into the light on the day of judgment.

11) **We would never know how to enter the kingdom of God.** All of mankind is born into the kingdom of darkness headed up by the evil one (1 John 5:18–19). We are blinded to our need for a savior which is why God draws us to Himself through the law in our hearts, conscience, natural revelation and the Spirit of God's conviction.

12) **We would never know a man's inability to get along with his fellow man.** Common sense leads us to the conclusion that this is an utter impossibility in spite of the political promises made by both parties. Consider eight billion people with the heart issues described by Jesus: "What comes out of a person is what defiles him. For from within, out of the heart of man, come evil thoughts, sexual immorality, theft, murder, adultery, coveting, wickedness, deceit, sensuality, envy, slander, pride, foolishness. All these evil things come from within, and they defile a person" (Mark 7:20–23).

13) **We would never know how to have peace in the midst of conflict.** As a friend of mine likes to say, all our decisions are driven by love or fear. The most quoted statement in Scripture is "fear not." Bill, peace comes from having an eternal perspective because believers have the assurance of eternal life. We don't have a midlife crisis because *there is no midpoint in that which is eternal.* This is not some pie-in-the-sky hope, but the reality of true joy, which comes from the spiritual confidence that God's grace is sufficient to see me through my earthly pilgrimage.

14) **We would never know the divine blueprint for marriage or what marriage represents.** In Genesis, we are told that "a man shall leave his father and his mother and hold fast to his wife, and they shall become one flesh" (2:24). The violation of this has caused massive problems in our society. In Ephesians, we are told that husbands are to "love your wives, as Christ loved the church and gave himself up for her"

(5:25). So marriage reflects the good news of the gospel. Christ died for me, and I should be willing to do the same for my wife.

15) **We would never know the value of life.** Bill, according to Genesis, man is made in the image and likeness of God (1:26). This is known as the *imago Dei*. It carries with it a vast domain of meaning, most importantly the ability to think, care, build relationships, and relate to God Himself. We have a mind, a will, and emotions. After the fall, this image was impaired by sin but not destroyed. In the New Heavens and the New Earth, the shattered image will be restored. The whole story of Scripture escorts the reader to this finality. God is King, and He rules in His sovereignty over all time and every molecule. And we read these words from the apostle Paul: "Have this mind among yourselves, which is yours in Christ Jesus, who, though he was in the form of God, did not count equality with God a thing to be grasped, but emptied himself, by taking the form of a servant, being born in the likeness of men. And being found in human form, he humbled himself by becoming obedient to the point of death, even death on a cross. Therefore God has highly exalted him and bestowed on him the name that is above every name, so that at the name of Jesus every knee should bow, in heaven and on earth and under the earth, and every tongue confess that Jesus Christ is Lord, to the glory of God the Father." Bill, we either bow now or later, but every knee will bow and every tongue will confess that Jesus Christ is Lord.

16) **We would never know why a man can't control his passions.** We have already hit on this topic by revealing the condition of the human heart. It has been said that the heart of the problem is the problem with the human heart.

Everyone wants to know why they can't have more self-control, so they purchase more self-help books but the issue is that *self* is the problem. The basic message of those books is that *you can do it*. Step up to the plate and be a man! You are the master of your fate and the captain of your soul! What your mind can conceive you can achieve! You can do anything you put your mind to! So I decided yesterday to bench seven-hundred pounds. It turns out the self-help philosophies did not live up to their promises . . .

17) **We would never know that God is sovereign, meaning He is in charge of all history.** God is omnipotent, which means He is all powerful, and He is omnipresent which means He is everywhere. This gives the believer great comfort. "Ah, Sovereign LORD, you have made the heavens and the earth by your great power and outstretched arm. Nothing is too hard for you" (Jer. 32:17). "Am I a God at hand, declares the LORD, and not a God far away? Can a man hide himself in secret places so that I cannot see him? declares the LORD. Do I not fill heaven and earth? declares the Lord" (Jer. 23:23–24).

18) **We would never know that Jesus Christ is coming again to usher in the New Heavens and the New Earth.** The Bible makes it abundantly clear that He is coming back to make "all things new" (Rev. 21:5). When is He coming? He tells us that "concerning that day and hour no one knows . . . but the Father only" (Matt. 24:36). But we also see that He is "coming soon" (Rev. 22:7), and the "time is near" (Rev. 22:10). We need to be ready.

19) **We would never know that what we don't know is infinitely more than what we do know.** That should humble us to the core. Both atheists and believers should take this into account. There are certain fields in which we double

our knowledge every year or two. Medicine and technology are at least two of those fields. However, that knowledge will never fix the human condition. In the prophetic book of Daniel we read these words: "But you, Daniel, shut up the words and seal the book, until the time of the end. Many shall run to and fro, and knowledge shall increase" (Dan. 12:4). Has there ever been a time when man increased so rapidly in knowledge than today? Yet we are still infinitely far from knowing all that God knows.

20) **We would never know what it means to be born again.** The gospel of John clearly reveals the meaning in the words of Jesus: "Truly, truly, I say to you, unless one is born again he cannot see the kingdom of God" (John 3:3). Bill, no doubt you have heard people refer to "born-again Christians." Here is a little bit of biblical insight. If you are not born again, you are not a Christian. If you are a Christian, then you are born again. All this expression means is that we have been born physically into this world, but we need a second birth to enter into the Kingdom of God.

21) **We would never know the Kingdom of God is upside-down living.** It goes completely against the grain of Wall Street and Madison Avenue, which are all about me and my stuff. But my stuff doesn't leave this world with me. You will never see a hearse pulling a U-Haul.

    a. "Whoever finds his life will lose it, and whoever loses his life for my sake will find it" (Matt. 10:39). These are some of the most powerful words ever spoken by Jesus. We are, by nature, all about numero uno. This becomes a selfish life and a dead-end street with endless disappointments. When our lives are surrendered to God's ways and will, we truly find life to its full abundance.

b. He who gives will get. "It is more blessed to give than to receive" (Acts 20:35). All of kingdom living goes against the grain of our natural passions and desires, but is where we find real life.

c. He who serves will lead. Another word from the Master leader says, "The greatest among you shall be your servant" (Matt. 23:11). Those who serve are the real leaders. My dad who retired as a three-star admiral, told me one day that the backbone of the Navy were the sailors and Chief petty officers.

d. He who humbles himself will be exalted. Humility is one of the greatest virtues that can be displayed by any human being. Why is this so? Because humble people are teachable and approachable. We feel safe with a humble leader. There is less conflict as humility greases the skids in times of potential stress.

22) **We would never know that salvation is a gift from God and cannot be earned through good works.** Bill, I know we have talked about this one, but I want to take just one more opportunity to share this good news with you. If you are dependent on your human goodness to achieve a right relationship with God, you will forever be frustrated, wondering just how good you need to be. The good news of the gospel is that you could never be good enough—but you don't need to be. Jesus Christ lived a perfect life in your place and offers that perfection as a gift to anyone who will accept the offer (Eph. 2:8–9). If you, or anyone reading this, are ready to believe that, then today is the day of salvation!

Other books by Mike Minter
Stay The Course published by B&H publishing
A Western Jesus published by B&H publishing
Tag Along published by Reston Bible Church

BACK COVER

The stories of the Bible have long been the fodder for jokes from talk-show hosts and comedians. And, let's be honest, some of those jokes are really funny. And many of the tales of Scripture can seem fantastic at first glance. But when you dive below the surface, you find an ocean full of truth, with a perfectly crafted narrative that tells one big story—the story of redemption.

The reality is that Christians, agnostics, atheists, and everyone else in between have to wrestle with questions about the existence of God and the existence of the universe. Did a divine being create everything that we see around us, or did it all happen by chance? Did life emerge from a primordial soup eons upon eons ago, or did a loving and holy Creator form Adam from the dust?

In this book, Pastor Mike Minter shares a "conversation" with agnostic comedian Bill Maher, who loves to poke fun at some of the "silly" stories of the Bible. Minter shows how the Scriptures point to eternal truth—truth that is confirmed by the broken and sinful world around us.

www.ingramcontent.com/pod-product-compliance
Lightning Source LLC
Chambersburg PA
CBHW051227120626
46547CB00013B/1541